Just '30s

10 YEARS OF CLASSICS AND DEPRESSION-ERA WONDERS

Published by

Krause Publications, a division of F+W Media, Inc.
700 East State Street • Iola, WI 54990-0001
715-445-2214 • 888-457-2873
www.krausebooks.com

To order books or other products call toll-free 1-800-258-0929
or visit us online at www.krausebooks.com or www.Shop.Collect.com

Library of Congress Control Number: 2010925548

ISBN-13: 978-1-4402-1428-8
ISBN-10: 1-4402-1428-X

Designed by Sharon Bartsch
Edited by Brian Earnest

Printed in the United States of America

CONTENTS

A DECADE OF GIANT STEPS

Think of the 1930s, and the first thing that comes to mind is The Great Depression. The nation was hurting, war was imminent overseas, and many Americans were just trying to weather the storm and hope for better days.

Ironically, however, when it comes to automobiles, the 1930s were one of our most memorable decades. Sure, many promising and established car companies became casualties of the suffocating economy, but the cars they left behind are some of the most important and most beautiful machines ever to roll off American assembly lines.

On the technical end of things, we welcomed the V-shaped engine block; V-8s, V-12s and V-16s were huge leaps forward from anything that had been offered on a big scale before. We also got smoother shifting transmissions, tempered glass, radios, hydraulic brakes and integrated trunk space.

Car bodies became more rounded and sophisticated looking. Fenders were no longer bolted-on appendages.

In the 1930s, automobiles weren't just simple contraptions that got us from Point A to Point B. The buying public demanded more stylish, comfortable and reliable machines, and the car companies delivered.

In the pages that follow, the editors and publisher of *Old Cars Weekly* and *Old Cars Report Price Guide* look back on some of the cars that we remember most from an amazing decade. There were dozens, perhaps hundrends, of great machines produced during that period, but we picked out a few that were worthy of feature stories, and worth remembering for what they were when they were new, and for how they are viewed by historians and old car hobbyists today.

By John Gunnell

A 'CAR GUY'S' CORD

Customized Cord L-29 was a Brooks Stevens favorite

The one-of-a-kind, black-and-cream L-29 Cord speedster once owned by Brooks Stevens is now fully restored to the way it was when the designer customized it in the mid-1930s. The Cord is now a part of the Schoenthaler Collection.

Several ago, when the Milwaukee (Wis.) Art Museum featured an exhibition spotlighting the work of industrial designer Brooks Stevens, one of the cars in the show was a beautiful 1930 Cord L-29 that Stevens had personalized for himself long ago. Stevens often told me this vehicle was a personal favorite among the many interesting vehicles he displayed in his museum in Mequon, Wis.

Stevens' product designs went from the Oscar Mayer Wienermobile to the wide-mouthed peanut butter jar. He even designed the AMF Roadmaster bicycle that I rode as a kid in the early '50s, and I have always kicked myself for not buying the mint example I found about 20 years ago. Ed Schoenthaler, of Downers Grove, Ill., did not repeat my mistake. Given the opportunity to buy Stevens' L-29 speedster in 1997, he and his wife, Judy, did exactly that.

Stevens was born in Milwaukee and

This is how the Hoffman X-8 looked back in the 1980s when on display in the Brooks Stevens Automotive Museum in Mequon, Wis. Both the front and rear doors are hinged at the center pillar.

studied architecture at Cornell University in New York from 1929-'33. His influence on transportation design included the design of motorcycles, trains and cars. While he didn't design the famous front-wheel-drive production car, he owned an L-29 Cord and had it restyled by the Cord Corp.s' Limousine Body Co.

Stevens was a car enthusiast from an early age. Over the years, he helped design cars of more than 50 brands. He was still a teenager when he went to a wedding in the early '30s. At that wedding, a Cord was given to the bride and groom. Stevens was impressed by the car and wanted to own one. Stevens' father was a successful engineer and he helped his son buy an L-29 Cord cabriolet in

1931, when it was about a two-year-old car.

From its beginning, the Cord L-29 was an innovative automobile. It was manufactured by a branch of the Cord Corp. that was named after founder E.L. Cord. The L-29 was introduced in 1929 as a 1930 model. The "L" part of the L-29 name originated in the Auburn Automobile Co.'s name for the front-wheel drive project while it was in its infancy (According to the book "Auburn & Cord," Auburn-Cord historian Stan Gilliland believes the "L" prefix was used for chassis orders). According to Ed Schoenthaler, the "29" stood for 1929. Race car builder Harry Miller, who built many front-wheel-drive race cars, consulted on the project's design work and offered his patents and manufacturing rights for a royalty for each car built. Miller worked with Cord Corp. engineer Cornelius Willett Van Ranst. John Oswald was the body engineer and worked under chief designer Al Leamy.

The L-29 Cord hit the market 30 days before the Ruxton, another front-wheel-drive car. Many changes had to be made in the original design before production actually started. A 298.6-cid Lycoming side-valve eight was used which, in stock format, developed 125 hp. Brooks Stevens loved to talk about the modifications he made to get the output of his up to about 150 hp. Attached to the engine was a three-speed manual transmission. The Cord did 0-to-60 mph in 20 seconds.

As a design student, Stevens became fascinated with the Cord's technology and performance, the latter being quite strong for

Hoffman Eight was last car in Stevens museum

While most cars from the Brooks Steven Automotive Museum were sold to private collectors in the years immediately following the designer's 1995 death, one car stuck around for a while. The last car to leave the museum was a streamlined sedan with an eight-cylinder radial engine made by Roscoe C. (Rod) Hoffman around 1934 or 1935.

Hoffman was about 47 when he designed this car. He graduated from Purdue University in 1911 with a degree in mechanical engineering. He started a company called Hoffman Motor Developments in 1934 in Detroit. Hoffman was an independent engineer and knew many people in the auto industry. He may have done projects for GM. Studebaker and Packard. He became a good friend of Brooks Stevens and gifted the car to him in 1961.

The car — now dubbed the Hoffman X-8 — is believed to have evolved from a deal that the French automaker Mathis was working on with Henry Ford. Apparently, Hoffman, Ford and Mathis got together to develop a radical X-engined car that was envisioned for European production. The prototype was constructed in Boston, Mass.

The all-steel Hoffman features a unitized body and frame with a honeycomb floor around the perimeter serving as strengthening members. It has a tubular front axle, front transverse leaf spring, front trailing arms and tube shocks all around.

The rear suspension features fully independent half shafts with Cardan joints at each end, along with longitudinal leaf springs and trailing arms. It has a 115-inch wheelbase and 181.35 overall length. It weighs in at about 3,100 lbs. and puts out 75 hp.

the day. About the time he graduated from Cornell in 1936, he decided to restyle the car. He patterned its appearance after that of the new Auburn speedster. His modifications included narrowing the body slightly and lowering the cowl line. At the rear, he discarded the stock rumble seat, smoothed the deck lid panel and added an airplane-like fin. He used a V-shaped windshield and raked it back for a sportier look.

Stevens redesigned the front fenders in a heavily valanced style that reflected the streamlining trend of the day. The Cord's six-wheel equipment was removed to eliminate the side-mounted spare tires. Mesh screens were used on the hood sides in a functional change that also helped cool the engine. The designer favored narrow Woodlites for headlamps and finished the car in a black-and-cream duo-tone that became a Stevens trademark over the ensuing years.

Inside the car, Stevens designed a new engine-turned instrument panel and worked in a luggage compartment beneath the rear deck panel. Storage access was by hinged seat backs. Since Stevens did not have facilities to build the car, he took his renderings to Limousine Body Co. and had them "factory customize" it.

Stevens' engine hop-ups included a dual-carb intake manifold and a special exhaust system. The rear axle gear ratios were changed. The Cord was finished in 1936 or 1937 and Stevens proceeded to drive it more than 140,000 miles until his death in 1995. The car was driven frequently and driven hard. It was even entered in numerous road races.

Many people were interested in the car when the Schoenthalers arranged to purchase it from the Stevens family in 1997. The Stevens family wanted the car to be kept as he designed it and hoped to see it at concours events, such as those in Pebble Beach, Calif.; Auburn, Ind.; and at Meadow Brook Hall in Michigan. "We took it to all three concours," Schoenthaler once said. "Now, we're trying to decide whether we should enter it in road races and competitive events."

Schoenthaler said the Cord was a "good 20-footer" when he bought it, because Stevens had made quick fixes anytime the car was bruised. The Schoenthalers had a nut-and-bolt restoration done, but made certain that everything was fixed exactly the way Brooks Stevens had it. Schoenthaler said that cars like the Stevens Cord are found by "Keeping your eyes and ears open; we get all the hobby publications and belong to dozens of clubs."

Although most of the cars formerly in the Brooks Stevens Automotive Museum are now privately owned, the Milwaukee Institute of Art and Design (MIAD) kept the designer's personal archives. It was donated to the Milwaukee Art Museum in 1997. The archives include original sketches, renderings, models and photos. The museum has made many of the objects from the archives available for viewing online at www.mam.org/brooksstevens.

MOPARS WERE STARS IN THE 1930S

In the first half of 1934, sales of Plymouths, like this town sedan, as well as De Sotos, were considered strong. At the mid-year point, officials declared that more than 45,000 Plymouths and De Sotos had been delivered by dealers.

Chrysler's rise to stardom amid the automotive galaxy of hopefuls occurred in the 1930s. Its rise was consistent, persistent, and a notable achievement during some of the worst economic years that ever plagued a nation.

The 1930s were not a great time to buy a new car if you didn't have an income or if your savings had vanished. Yet, it was the best of times to buy a car, since innovation, design, and quality features abounded at what would normally have been considered attractive prices. In effect, luxury car features were becoming cheaper and were applied to more mid- and low-priced cars.

Officials with Chrysler were proud to offer its entire range of cars and trucks hitting all price ranges. Heated promotion

In 1940, Dodge, as well as other Chrysler brands, was marketing its vehicles to women by pointing out the cars' comfort innovations.

revolved around Plymouth, Dodge, and De Soto, since these were in the more affordable ranges in the 1930s.

Walter P. Chrysler was an engineer at heart, a real tool man who liked to tinker with cars, as well as ideas on how to build and market them. His leadership of the corporation bearing his name was very important, since it lent the image of rugged reliability and trustworthy performance to any car he sanctioned. More than that, he was desired for other positions rather than just father of the Chrysler Corporation. In 1934, he was asked to join the board of directors of New York Central Railroad. The elected position was a natural, since Chrysler had made his mark early in life as a railroad man in Kansas. Helping a railroad in the 1930s was an indirect way to help the weakened car industry, since much of the raw material and vendor-produced compo-

nents traveled to factories by rail. Completed cars also went by rail to their appointed sales outlets.

He could afford to share his time and ideas. De Soto was doing well. In July of 1934, production was on schedule. Retail deliveries in the first five months of that year totaled 9,276 units. That was a 17 percent increase over the similar period in 1933.

Plymouth was no slouch in the win column, either. An industry expert noted in mid 1934 that "De Soto dealers have delivered 45,701 De Sotos and Plymouths since the first of the year." De Soto had a special honor, too. It was awarded the Grand Prix and Premier Prix honors in the aerodynamic class at the annual Concours d' Elegance at Monte Carlo. Since its design was of the Airflow school, this had to have made Chrysler officials break into smiles. They were, after all, risking the company's future on the new styling trend. With the awards plus solid sales, it looked like the idea was a winner.

As for Plymouth, production was running close to 1,900 units a day as orders ran ahead of production. In fact, a new all-time record was acknowledged for June 19, 1934, when 1,898 units left the assembly line that single day. The industry took note. All this was especially poignant, since Plymouth was a relative newcomer to the skyline of America's automotive luminaries. It entered production in 1928.

Plymouth was the contender in the low-price field against sales heavyweights Chevrolet and Ford. It did not carry Airflow styling, but was more sedate and predictable in an evolutionary rather than revolutionary manner. Still, it was good car for the money and was hitting its marketing target.

To augment Plymouth's image, motion picture stars and race track figures were signed to appear on the silver screen in company promotions. The Plymouth film "Death Cheater's Holiday" included James McBride and Al St. John, both well-known stage performers. Also on the screen were Barney Oldfield of racing fame, plus Harry Hartz and Billy Arnold, names commonly connected with speedway successes.

Dodge was doing very well, too, thank you. Retail deliveries in nearly the first half of 1934 amounted to 62,627 passenger cars and trucks. This was an increase of 91 percent over the same period in 1933. The brand's biggest week to date ended June 9, 1934, with 5,226 passenger cars and trucks delivered.

Mr. Chrysler was justified in the purchase of Dodge Brothers on July 30 of 1928. It was a case of a smaller company swallowing a larger operation, but the big gulp proved wise. Dodge may have lasted through the Depression of the 1930s because of its substantial and strong dealer network, reputation, and great engineering. But we cannot be as certain whether the Chrysler line or its companions would have made it through the stormy sky of that decade had not Dodge been beaming with success.

This became a reality when the hype over Airflow styling subsided and winds of disinterest seemed to blow through the sales market. The Airflow style was not endearing as many buyers as Mr. Chrysler had hoped. It was a costly venture, and for a time, it seemed the cash loss and heavy investment in tooling and manufacturing was an impassable planetary blockade. More than that, it almost brought down Chrysler's entire sky.

Dodge, like Plymouth, did not venture forth with Airflow design, but stuck with evolutionary principles. By 1939, the entire Chrysler Corp. had become much more predictable and downright conservative in its own right, albeit overall styling cues were clear enough to distinguish any car in its lines as having Chrysler heritage.

Dodge for 1940 was attracted to women as a sales influence. So were other car makers. Chrysler cars were often seen as a man's car, but the influence of women on the market gradually shifted this thinking. What was it that Dodge offered to make women vote for the cars?

One reporter analyzed the 1940 Dodge line by saying, "Windows and doors are sealed against weather and dirt." Yes ma'am, that was a plus for women who wanted to be secure, comfortable, and clean. "All car controls are directly in front of the driver behind the steering wheel and out of the way." Another plus for women who liked controls that were handy and logical. "The cowl ventilator has three variations of opening and a rain trap." Okay, this provided more control for free air intake to the passenger compartment, which meant a woman in a dress (who could feel the air movement more than a man with trousers) would be more prone to control the flow. And heaven forbid that rain should enter the car or wet the carpet!

The reach of a man was often longer than a woman's in 1940, so "radio buttons are handy to the steering wheel so that a driver alone need not reach to change stations." This kept the woman driver in control of the wheel and removed the risk of fighting the wheel while changing stations. Since radio had become a hot option by 1940, this was an important factor.

"Gear levers have a shorter throw and move easily and surely," said the reporter, another check in the plus column. "Electric windshield wipers are on deluxe models." Another plus.

For women who were riding in the rear seat, it was noted there was a small, "well thought out" point. It was "a drain slot in the rear quarter window molding to catch drips from partly opened pivoting wing windows." That removed the nuisance of drips on the arms of riders or on the nice upholstery, thus making it damp and avoidable if milady was in a fancy outfit.

Vision was improved. Seats were more comfortable. Legroom was ample, "and a parcel shelf is behind the sedan rear seat," a nice feature for the woman who had a small item to store temporarily and did not want to lift the trunk lid. Mirrors were tinted with color to guard against glare from cars behind. "Warning tell-tale lights on the instrument panels report adverse operating conditions," it was noted. In other words, women or men who were not mechanically minded did not have to fully understand the sounds or trouble signs as much as simply look for the warning lights.

As for Chryslers, experts noted women would adore the beautiful clean styling "with very smooth exterior and large luggage space concealed in the rear. The cars have a great deal of space inside, resulting from a 122-1/2-inch wheelbase, and have large, deep seats, all between the axles,

1930 Chrysler Model 70 Coupe

from which all vision is excellent... Plastic-decorated instrument panel will catch many an eye.

"Ladies will like silent operation resulting from improved mechanical parts super-finishings, and the liberal use of rubber."

In 1939, when the 1940 Plymouth was introduced, it was considered a big car with a 117-1/2-inch wheelbase. "Body styling is completely new, smooth, and unified from front to rear;" just the thing for a well-dressed and perfectly coordinated lady to appreciate. The frame was larger and heavier, which allowed for stiffness and more room inside. "Curved rear window is a style note which has a practical value in giving more rearward vision... rear seats are three inches wider at the hip line for greater

comfort," but the reporter did not even hint that ladies should be more conscious of bigger hips.

When Chrysler Corp. waved goodbye to the 1930s, it had to have been done with mixed feelings. Gone were the early versions of the Plymouth and De Soto. The Airflow was a memory most company execs preferred to forget. Refinements and market realizations redirected the rise of company products toward a wider market. Luxury was more important. So was styling. Truly, the car market for America was radically different in 1930 versus 1939.

By 1939, the names Chrysler, Dodge, Plymouth, and De Soto had become fixed points in the American car galaxy and would remain so for years to come.

TO PARADE & SERVE
San Francisco PD remains original owner of '31 Lincoln

This 1931 Lincoln Model K Sport Touring is believed to be oldest in-service
police vehicle in California. The largely original car still retains its six-volt
electro-mechanical siren, and is still registered as an emergency vehicle
by the San Francisco Police Department, which bought it new.

Having served the citizens of San Francisco for more than 70 years, this 1931 Lincoln Model K Sport Touring is believed to be the oldest in-service police vehicle in the state of California.

According to OldCarsReport.com, this unrestored touring is 1 of 3,540 Lincolns manufactured that year, and one of four Lincolns purchased by the city of San Francisco. This particular seven-passenger Sport Touring was used by the city's police department as official transportation for its chief of police. Retail price of this Depression-era Lincoln was about $4,400 — or about the price of 10 Fords. Only 45 of this model, designated Model 203 by the manufacturer, were built.

Lincolns of the era were fast and pow-

The Lincoln hood ornament is a popular target for thieves.

erful, and thus a favorite of the police, as well as the gangsters they chased. Powering this approximately 5,000-lb. touring is a 385-cid L-head (side-valve) V-8 engine. For 1931, a bump in compression to 4.95:1 and state-of-the-art carburetion technology — improved intake manifolding and a two-barrel downdraft carburetor — increased horsepower from 90 in 1930 to 120 hp in 1931. Power is transmitted through a three-speed manual transmission equipped with Synchromesh on second and third gears. The car also features free-wheeling, another innovation introduced on Lincolns that year. This combination gives the heavy touring a top speed of about 90 mph, but considering the hilly terrain of San Francisco, it is highly doubtful that such a top speed was ever achieved in the SFPD's car, nor was the free-wheeling feature likely utilized. (Free-wheeling was a short-lived feature intended

for gas saving which disconnected the engine from the drivetrain and did not allow engine braking in some prewar cars.)

While on the subject of brakes, cable-operated Bendix Duo Servo mechanical brakes handled stopping chores. Other options include a Philco AM radio receiver, an electric Seth-Thomas clock mounted on the instrument panel and dual sidemounts.

William J. Quinn, known to be innovative and progressive, served as San Francisco's police chief from 1929-'40. He utilized the chauffeur-driven dual-cowl Lincoln as his official transportation until 1937. The stock six-volt electrical system is still utilized and adequately powers the twin red cowl-mounted emergency lamps and electro-mechanical "growler" siren.

After the police department retired the Lincoln from active service, the department parked it in the basement of its main po-

One of the few features of the Lincoln that has been restored is the upholstery. The instrument cluster and the steering wheel appear original to the car.

The Lincoln Model K 385-cid, 60-degree flathead V-8 develops 120 hp and is capable of propelling the heavy touring car up to 90 mph with the standard 4.23:1 rear-end ratio. Optional ratios of 4.58:1 and 4.90:1 would increase acceleration and lower top speed.

lice building, reserving it for special events, such as parades. One foggy, windy day in May 1937, the Lincoln was the lead vehicle when the Golden Gate Bridge officially opened. It has also transported mayors and former mayors of San Francisco, along with other dignitaries, such as President Franklin D. Roosevelt.

In its nearly eight decades of service to the city, the Lincoln has accumulated 66,600 miles and is still in original condition, save for some re-upholstery and replacement carpeting. According to Sgt. Richard Lee, who is currently in charge of SFPD Fleet Services, the only modifications to the old touring are painted steel plates mounted outside the sidemount spare tires in order to affix magnetic department insignias. An electric fuel pump was also installed to combat vapor-lock issues.

Another issue to contend with is the radiator cap/ornament — which is an attraction to thieves. Sgt. Lee had an original ornament meticulously reproduced along with a spare "just in case" the original walked away. To be on the safe side, when the Lincoln is parked, Lee keeps the radiator cap securely locked inside his office until the car is called for duty, once again, for a parade.

A WEE WONDER

1932 Austin is huge fun in the smallest of packages

**Bob and Cathy Cunningham are big fans of little cars,
and their pride and joy is their 1932 Austin-American Roadster.**

Back in the mid-1970s, Bob Cunningham came up with a unique way for choosing a car and charting his course in the old car hobby. The Des Moines, Iowa, resident was no stranger to the world of old cars – he bought his first car, a 1936 Chevy, at the age of 15, and went on to own a 1927 Willys and '52 Packard, so he hadn't played favorites when it came to picking cars.

But being a bit of a bantamweight himself, Cunningham started to think maybe he needed to match his cars to his own stature. "Well, at that time I was 120 lbs., and if I had a dead battery or broke down on the road, that was a lot weight to push around," he said. "I decided to make a list of all the aesthetic qualities I wanted in a car, and then try to find them in the smallest car possible. That's what led me to buy my first Bantam roadster in 1976."

Cunningham says he took his wife, Cathy, who has turned into his equal as a American-Austin/Bantam buff, on their honeymoon in the roadster in 1980. Their destination: their first Bantam club meet. Since then, the couple's marriage has been a match made in micro-car heaven. The Cunninghams have gone on to immerse themselves in the quirky, undersized world of Bantams and American-Austins and have served as the editors for the American Austin Bantam Club News publication for many years. They have both become authorities on the history of their favorite little cars and the proud owners of this 1932 American Austin roadster.

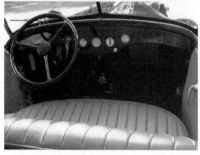

They Cunninghams don't drive the pint-sized roadster on the highway as much as they used to, but the car is still pretty much a daily driver for their shorter excursions in and around Des Moines. And regardless of how short the trips are, the little car with the seemingly oversized wheels never fails to illicit a reaction from other motorists.

"People think it's a kit car, because it's so little and cute," Cathy said. "A lot of people see this type of car somewhere … W.C. Field used it in one of his movies, and a lot of them were used as prop cars in the movies."

Indeed, while they never really caught on with the buying public, didn't enjoy a long production run, and were destined to become orphans at a young age, the American Austins certainly didn't lack personality. With almost cartoonish proportions, tiny 75-inch wheelbases, disc wheels, fat-looking tires and a high ground clearance (8 3/4 inches), they certainly had a look all their own. The cars were only 10 feet long, 4 feet, 4 inches wide and weighed in at about 1,100 lbs. Looking a little like a fattened-up pedal car, American Austins frequently turned up in films of the day, with celebrities like Buster Keaton, Ernest Hemmingway and the Our Gang kids all being seen crowded into their cozy confines.

American Austin was founded in 1929 and produced cars from 1930-'34 in Butler Pa. The total production run during that time period was only about 20,000 cars. The company went into receivership in 1932 and production was halted in 1935-'37, but re-started again from 1938-'41 under the American Bantam banner. Bantam, of course, became legendary for its efforts in designing the first military Jeeps, but the contracts to build the rugged new vehicles for the government eventually went to Willys and Ford, and Bantam quietly disappeared for good in 1941.

The Cunninghams estimate that only about 100 of the American Austin roadsters survive, and probably only 300 to 350 American Austins of any kind remain, counting the various coupes the company also built from 1930-'34. "We had about 80 cars show up at a meet in 2005, which is pretty amazing when you consider how many are probably left," Cathy noted.

Still, even considering its rarity, the Cunninghams have no qualms about treating their car as it was intended — as practical, reliable no-frills transportation.

"My husband is not afraid to drive it. He will take it out frequently in the summer," Cathy said. "I don't drive it because you have to double clutch, and I've never quite gotten the hang of it. We've had other people who drive old cars who have tried to drive and they couldn't... But once you master it, it's quite a fun little car.

"It's a good little driver. We take it to nationals and so on, and there is always a 20- to 25-mile road tour, and it runs just fine for those times ... The roadster has no heater in it, but because there is little insulation between you and the engine, you stay quite warm. I always thought the best weather for these roadsters is about 50 degrees."

But Bob draws the line when it comes to getting out on the highway. If it was possible to "underpower" a car that weighed only 1,100 lbs., American Austin was apparently able to do it. Under the hood is a 45-cubic-inch, water-cooled, L-head four-cylinder engine that kicks out about 12 hp, driven by a three-speed. With a top speed of about 45 mph, the car isn't exactly traveling in the passing lanes out on the Interstate.

"It's a lot of fun, but I have to look in my rearview mirror a lot, especially when leaving stoplights," Bob said. "People expect such a small car to be peppy, but it takes a while to get up to speed ... Most people probably wouldn't be driving it in a city of 500,000 people, but I've been driving them for 30 years, so I'm pretty used to it. I just don't drive it on the highway anymore. I don't get respect from people that I need with it. People tend to ride up on your bumper."

"When you get two people in car on slight hill, you kind of feel like, 'Should I get out and walk?'" Cathy added with a laugh. "I remember one time we trailered it to a river rally, it was fine going in, but then coming out we were crawling probably 5 miles up the hills coming out. I thought, 'It might help and be faster if just got out and walked.'"

In the end, the lack of power, and no doubt its overall diminutive size, were enough to doom the American Austins and Bantams. The idea of a small economy car was still a bit of a foreign concept in the 1930s, and though the cars were certainly conversation pieces and attracted their share of attention, few customers wanted to take one home.

By Byron Olsen

THE BERGHOLT STREAMLINE CAR

Trailblazer for aerodynamic automobiles

**The Streamline is the product of Fred Bergholt, a Minneapolis resident
who wanted a car that was as aerodynamic as an airplane.**

The biggest design news in the entire field of transportation during the 1930s was, without a doubt, streamlining. The streamline movement forever changed not just automobiles, but other forms of transportation, architecture and most manufactured goods that were part of everyday life. Everything from trains to toasters got totally restyled in the '30s as a result of the acceptance of the concepts of streamlining. This is the story of a unique streamlined automobile designed and built by a visionary man from Minneapolis named Fred Bergholt, who built his dream in 1932, at the very dawn of the streamline age.

Streamlining burst on the scene, seemingly all over the world at once, in 1933 and '34. Those two years saw the introduction of the first popular and successful high-speed lightweight streamlined train, the Burlington Zephyr. On the automotive scene, a number of radical streamlined concept cars appeared at such places as the Chicago Century of Progress Exposition. One of these concept

Inside the cockpit, occupants of the Streamline can enjoy a luxurious environment, complete with fold-out windshield sections and map pockets in the door panels.

The rear passenger compartment of the big two-door sedan features a large seat, side lamps and map pockets. The split rear window is similar to the Pierce-Arrow Silver Arrow.

From the rear, the Streamline shows the fastback styling that became popular years after the car was constructed.

cars by designer John Tjaarda became the prototype for the Lincoln-Zephyr, which was put in production in 1936. In Europe, there was much activity as well. The Volkswagen Beetle made its first appearance, as did the revolutionary rear-engined Czech Tatra. In the United States, the aerodynamic Chrysler Airflow was introduced in 1934.

Interest in smoothing the contours of moving objects such as trains and autos was inspired by the infant aviation industry. Airplanes had to move with the absolute minimum of wind resistance, or they simply would not have enough power to be able to maintain air speed. Interest in aviation was crystallized by Lindberg's solo non-stop flight from New York to Paris in 1927. From that point on, airplane-inspired streamlining became the wave of the future. After a five-year gestation period, streamlining burst on

the scene from all directions in 1933.

One of the significant new automobile designs that first appeared in January 1933 at the New York Auto Show was the Pierce-Arrow Silver Arrow. This was a trailblazing new design on a Pierce-Arrow V-12 chassis. Only six were built, as the real purpose was to present new design concepts. The roof line was a racy fastback, and it was one of the first cars designed in America with full fender design, that made the fenders an integral part of the body and extended them the entire length of the car. This design provided room for the spare tire carriers to be entirely enclosed within the body sides just behind the front wheels. The body sides extended out to the full width of the car, completely covering the running boards. It was a stunning car and became the talk of the town.

What Pierce-Arrow and New Yorkers

didn't know was that, for at least a month before the Silver Arrow was introduced, a car had been running on the streets of far-away Minneapolis, which bore an uncanny resemblance to the Silver Arrow. It was the Bergholt Streamline, an innovative new car designed by Fred Bergholt and built under his direction. The Bergholt car had the same sloping front end, the same fastback rear, and sides that enclosed even more of the fenders than the Pierce. The spare tire was even concealed in the front fender, just like the Silver Arrow. How did such a coincidence come about?

At a time when nearly all automobiles sported open front fenders, the Streamline had enclosed fenders that sloped from the windshield to the front bumper.

Fred Bergholt was an inventive, creative guy who became interested in aviation in the 1920s. He and his brother actually built and sold gliders and then airplanes for a time. After 1927, Fred began thinking about designing a car.

His aircraft experience led him from the start to seek an innovative new shape that would move through the air smoothly like an airplane. He came up with two inspirations, both inspired by animals. He concluded that the turtle was one of the most aerodynamic, as well as hydrodynamic, forms in nature. Whether swimming or walking, water or air flows off the turtle's back without encumbrance. In promoting his car design later, Bergholt made much use of his turtle inspiration.

The other inspiration from nature was the hammerhead shark, which inspired Fred to make the body larger at the front and tapering down at the rear. Both of these design concepts are found to various degrees in the work of other early streamline designers. The basic tear-drop shape, often a streamline design objective, is a good example. Bergholt's concepts are very similar to those advocated by Leon Jaray, a pioneering European advocate of automotive aerodynamics in the '20s.

Bergholt bought a new 1932 Ford V-8 sedan and removed the body. A metal worker named Edgar Lantz then went to work to shape a new metal body to Fred's design. But before work began, Fred took out several patents on the unique design features of the Bergholt Streamline (his choice of name for the car). Many years later, after Fred contended that other car builders were using his design ideas, litigation resulted in a settlement in which

One of the significant new automobile designs that first appeared in January 1933 at the New York Auto Show was the Pierce-Arrow Silver Arrow. Looking very similar to it was the Streamline, which beat the Silver Arrow's styling by one year.

Fred felt he had been vindicated.

The car was completed in 1932, well before the Silver Arrow. Fred subsequently showed it to several auto companies, but none were interested. Bergholt claimed they all thought it was too far ahead of its time and that he should come see them again in five years! After that, the Streamline was put to work promoting the family cosmetics business, where it rang up over 200,000 miles and went through three engines! Fred claimed that the slippery body let the car and engine run so fast that engine bearings burned out.

In Fred's later years, the family fortunes turned for the worse, and the Streamline languished in storage. After Bergholt died in 1978, the family turned the car over to a good friend Harlow Loney, who has cared for the car ever since. In 1993, Loney began a complete restoration of the Streamline, a process that took 10 years. Today, the Streamline looks better, and is in better condition than it has been since it was built. The 1932-vintage Ford V-8 runs great, and the entire interior has been beautifully redone. Standing close to the car is a reminder of how foresighted Fred Bergholt was. The sides flair out dramatically, reminding one of the ground effects spoilers on modern performance cars. The wind-cheating, sloping front end, the concealed running boards and the spare tire well concealed inside the front fender are all reminders of Fred's creative genius.

By Brian Earnest

A 'FORD GUY'S' CHEVY

1932 Confederate sedan was too sweet to pass up

The "Confederate" moniker was applied to Chevrolet's 1932-model-year cars and included 14 different body styles and seating arrangements.

In official company nomenclature, it was known as the 1932 Chevrolet Model 21BA Confederate Special Sedan. Hal Hartel and his wife Beth just casually call it "the Chevy." As in, "Honey, I need to run down to the store for a loaf of bred, should I just take the Chevy?"

"And she calls it her 'Bonnie and Clyde car, too" adds Hal with a laugh.

The Hartels, who live in Yorktown, Va., both chuckle at the notion of their superb specimen being "just a Chevy," but Hal justifies the term "because I'm a Ford guy! Actually, I tease Beth that it's her car, not mine. I've always been a Ford man!"

But the Hartels were in agreement when it came time to pull the trigger and buy their lovely sedan eight years ago when it

unexpectedly went up for sale. The couple had been involved with the car hobby previously with a 1967 Mustang, and they also have a unique 1928 GMC firetruck, but a '32 Confederate sedan was a whole different animal.

"Actually, a friend of ours had pictures of the car that he was showing around," Hal recalled. "The car was his neighbor's and he wanted to sell it, and we have kind of an informal cruise here on Saturday nights and he wanted to know if I knew anybody that might be interested in it. I said, 'Yeah, we might be,' so the wife and I went over and looked at it, and she thought it would be a good investment.

"I said, 'Sure Dear!'"

If nothing else, the venerable sedan has been an investment in fun for the Hertels. They frequently take it to hobby events, weekend joy rides, and even used it in their son's wedding. The classic black paint job is accented by light-yellow wheels and white-sidewall tires which, together with the car's liberal amount of shiny chrome, make it hard to ignore wherever it goes. "It's got its Senior award from the AACA, and we do some local shows with it," said Hal. "But what I usually do is put a sign in it that says 'Do Not Judge.' We're so involved with everything and with our charities, we're not really into [judging]… That's not why I go to car shows, anyway.

"We just really like the early-'30s stuff. To me, it's a very classy car. Even with the hot rods and stuff, I still like the early-'30s cars."

The "Confederate" moniker was applied to Chevrolet's 1932-model-year cars and included 14 different body styles and seating arrangements. Only three of those were four-door cars, with the Special Sedan be-

ing the second-most popular choice among all 14 Chevrolets with 52,446 units built —behind only the two-door Coach.

The '32s had some noteworthy styling updates over the previous year, including the prominent door-type hood louvers that were chrome on the Deluxe models. Also new for the year was a longer hood design, deeper-crowned fenders, a downdraft carburetor, additional frame cross member, and a counter-balanced crankshaft. Other standard features included a tilting windshield, a built-in sun visor and an adjustable seat.

The engine was the familiar "Stovebolt" inline 194-cubic-inch six-cylinder that produced 60 hp. The wheelbase was 109 inches and the car rolled on 18 x 5.24 tires mounted on spoked wheels.

Options for the model year included front and rear bumpers, single and double sidemounts, heater, cowl lights, dual wipers, mirrors and metal tire covers. Standard equipment on the upscale Deluxe models included two ashtrays, assist cords, armrests, curtains for the quarter windows and a vanity case. The Hartels' car is equipped with the twin sidemounts, and with its two horns up front, it has a lot of curb appeal.

The car has just 69,000 miles on its odometer. An extended stay as a car dealer showpiece has no doubt preserved the Confederate and helped it remain in such good shape. "As far as the body and interior, it's had a fairly good life," Hal said. "For about 35 years, it sat inside a Chevy dealership. The father had it inside the showroom for years, and when he turned the business over to his son, the son didn't want it in the

showroom anymore… Other than that, the only thing we really know is that when we put the tags on it, they told us the car had spent the majority of its life in Virginia. They aren't allowed to tell you much… But it's pretty much an original.

"The guy I bought it from had it for about five years. The interior and body were in real good shape and I haven't done anything to that. We've had the pan off … Did the Babbitt bearings on it, and we've given it a tune-up and valve job. She's got about 69,000 on her and until recently we used it almost every weekend."

The Chevrolet isn't quite as challenging to drive as the couple's 19-foot firetruck, but it still requires some effort and caution. "It's funny — when you stick your arm out to turn left, everybody thinks you're waving at them," Hal laughed. "And it only has the one brake light on it. I've had people yell, 'Hey, your brake lights aren't working.'

Even boxing legend George Foreman was impressed with the Hartels' '32.

"You've gotta be aware of your surroundings. You gotta drive more slowly and be more aware. It takes two or three times longer to slow down than a modern car. It's still got mechanical brakes on it. It does fairly good [on the road]... It's not a car you want to push on the Interstate, but it will cruise all day at 30-35 mph ... we have a lot of fun with that car, it gets a lot of thumbs-up."

Hal and Beth both take their turns behind the wheel, "but I tend to drive it more," Hal said. One of those trips was to a car gathering that included former heavyweight boxing champion George Foreman, who took a shine to the Hartels' Chevrolet. "They were doing a promotion for one of the Midas dealers here, and he came over and got into the car. There were lots of cars there, and for him to come over and pick out our car, that was pretty neat."

Hal said even the mohair interior remains original, but that has never deterred the Hartels from putting some fun miles on the Confederate. "None of my cars has million-dollar paint jobs on them, or anything. They are drivers," he said.

And even if Hal and Beth ever decide they've had "the Chevy" long enough, they already have the next owners lined up. "My wife says one of my problems is I don't ever sell anything," Hal said. "But we have five grandkids, and only four cars, so we need one more."

SMASHING NASH
Refreshing a stunning, one-of-a-kind
Second Series 1932 Nash becomes a labor of love

The body of this 1932 Nash was built by the Seaman Body Corp.
It has dual sidemount spare tires and five louvers on each side of the hood.

During the late 1990s, Neil Maken, a Southern California car collector and the editor of *Skinned Knuckles* magazine, visited a local museum. He was driving his newly acquired 1949 Riley Saloon. The Riley captured the attention of the museum's owner, and he immediately offered to purchase it from Maken.

The Riley, having just arrived from Australia, was not yet documented, which involves scheduling a California Highway Patrol examination. Without the proper documentation, the Riley could not be registered, and so it could not be resold. Maken promised that, when it was registered, he would return to the museum. Several weeks

later, with his newly acquired DMV paperwork, Maken again visited the museum. The museum owner's ardor hadn't faded, but Maken was getting to enjoy the Riley and wasn't that anxious to sell. But when the museum owner offered a trade, Maken listened. In the end, Maken signed over the registration on the Riley and drove away in a 1932 Nash Second Series 1073 convertible sedan.

All that the museum could tell about the Nash was that it was purchased from another collector along with two other cars. It had recently come into the United States from somewhere in South America.

What was not known at the time was that the Nash was built in Kenosha, Wis., for export in 1932 to Argentina, lived in that country all of its life, and was the only known existing example of that body style in a right-hand-drive configuration. Argentina was a right-hand-drive country until

after the war. In 1945, it converted to the more common left-hand-drive roads and automobiles.

A crash course in Nash

1932, of course, was in the midst of the Great Depression. But despite the tight economy, Nash president E.H. McCarty was an optimist. His 1931 line of cars was successful. Nash earned almost $5 million in fiscal year 1931 and held slightly more than 2 percent of the total car market. The styling and engineering carried into the 1932 models. But in March of the 1932 model year, he switched over to a second series of cars. The Nash lineup included a flathead six-cylinder, a flathead eight-cylinder and two overhead-valve eight models. Within each category was a range of body styles. Nash's second series included slightly more horsepower, a longer wheelbase and a "tweaking" of the first series' cosmetics.

Above, the original trunk sits above the beavertail is backed by a chromed spring steel bumper. Below, the softness or firmness of the ride can be controlled by the driver.

The overhead-valve models, the 1080 and 1090 series, were now available with worm drive, and a four-door convertible was added to the larger car selection.

The 1931 lineup was designated as the 800 series – the six-cylinder models were the 860 series (the final digit varied indicating the body style), the flathead eight was the 870 series, and there were the two overhead-valve, dual-ignition series: The 880 and 890. 1932 meant only a change in the numbering, from the 800s to the 900s. There were the 960s, 970s, 980s and 990s.

The latter half of 1932, with the Second

Above, the rearview mirror with a clock is an add-on accessory.
Below, the art deco look is very evident on the instrument panel. A period-correct
radio has been mounted in the car, under the dash, with the control head
adjacent to the steering column.

The chrome flying bird mascot is similar to those used on other marques, but is distinctive in design and gracefulness.

Series of '32s, meant a new numbering sequence in mid-model year. The six-cylinders became the 1060s, the flathead eights were now 1070s and so forth. Despite dismal sales through the entire new-car market, Nash made money in 1932 — the only company other than General Motors to do so. Nash still retained 1.85 percent of new-car registrations. (The Second Series carried over into 1933 with yet another numbering change to the 1160s, 1170s, etc.).

Based on continuing good sales, the Nash selection of body styles was enormous. The 1932 First Series had five wheelbase lengths, from a 114-inch wheelbase for the six-cylinder to a 116-inch wheelbase for the flathead eight, as well as a 121-, 124- and a 133-inch wheelbase available on larger models. The Second Series was lengthened considerably: the six-cylinder jumped to a 116-inch, the flathead eight to 121-inch and from there to a 128-, 133- and a 142-inch wheelbase. The flathead-eight (1070) Second Series included a four-door sedan (Model 1070); a two-door, two-passenger coupe (1072); a two/four-passenger two-door coupe (1072R); a town sedan (1077); a convertible roadster (1071); and a five-passenger convertible sedan (1073).

The hunt for unique Nash parts

It is this last model, the flathead-eight

The passenge door opens wide to give easy access to the rear-seat passengers.
The front passenger seat folds forward, making access to the rear easy and comfortable.

Second Series 1073, that Maken acquired in the exchange. Sitting on a 121-inch wheelbase, the eight-cylinder engine displaced 247.4 cubic inches with 85 brake hp at 3,200 rpm. It has nine main bearings and a Stromberg EE-22 downdraft carburetor. (The first series has a 227.2 cid with 78 hp at 3,200 rpm.) The transmission is a standard three-forward, one-reverse-speed unit with a free-wheeling unit attached.

Having lived in Argentina for more than 50 years, and judging from its condition, the Nash was being used regularly, and maintenance consisted of doing whatever was possible to keep the thing running. Replacement parts were almost impossible to find in Argentina, and quite difficult in the United States. (Less than 5,000 of the engines of the type in Maken's car were produced in late 1932 to 1933). Nash had a reputation for making its own parts that were unique to its cars and to a specific model year. The EE-22 carburetor, for example, was used only on the 1932-'33 Nash 1070/1170 series, a couple of 1932-'34 Franklins and the 1932 Oldsmobile eight. The dual-point distributor was used only on Nash flathead eight models of 1931, '32 and '33.

When Maken acquired his Nash, it did not have the correct carburetor, it only had a single set of ignition points, and it did not have the correct steering wheel controls, light switches, horn, air cleaner, generator and a number of other components. But even more serious were a number of inter-

nal cracks in the block, allowing coolant to flow out and empty the cooling system after about 10 miles of driving. Driving the car home from the museum on that first day meant regular stops at filling stations along the way to replenish coolant.

The members of the Nash Car Club of America were extremely helpful in locating original specifications, part numbers and even helped in the acquisition of mechanical and chassis parts from a dismantled 1931 Nash.

The engine, however, was a serious problem. Maken was elated to locate a 1932 Nash eight-cylinder engine 3,000 miles from his home and was assured it was intact, had run when taken out of the car and was in excellent condition. Upon receipt, it turned out that the engine had thrown a rod, and that a plate was welded to the side of the block. It didn't make sense to rebuild it. Fortunately, about a year later, another block that was completely disassembled was located in the Washington state area. Between the original engine, the thrown-rod engine and the third one, rebuilder Jerry Washburn was able to make one good engine from all of the parts.

The load of mechanical parts acquired for the car included a steering column light switch, steering wheel with center controls, a horn and a number of other hard-to-find parts. The transmission was rebuilt with the help of several salvaged transmissions from similar year Nashes, as was the free-wheel-

The front of the car sports a plentitude of chrome: the two chrome Stabilite headlamp buckets, the chrome headlamp bar, the chrome grille and bumper, the two accessory Trippe lights, and the chrome flying bird radiator mascot.

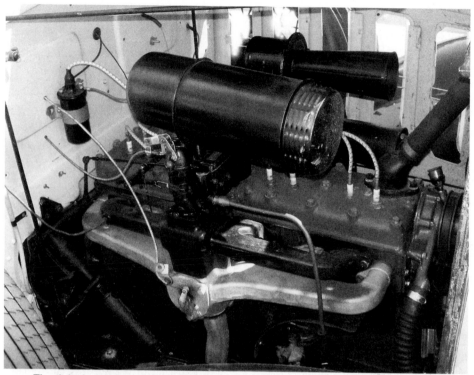

The right-hand view of the engine shows the carburetor, air cleaner/flame arrestor, manifolds and right-hand-drive steering column. The left-side view shows the generator, oil filter and starter motor, as well as two horns. The lower horn is the original diaphragm horn. The upper horn is an "ooh-gah" horn added for fun.

ing unit. The rear end was in good condition, needing just a cleaning and new gaskets and oil. Coker Tire was able to match the tires for the car.

But the rarity of parts was still to bite Maken. On a local trip, the car stopped dead in its tracks. It turned out to be a broken rear left axle shaft. That particular axle shaft was used only on the 1932-'33 six and flathead-eight Nashes, and not a single replacement seemed to be available. A replacement axle shaft was fabricated from a spare right shaft, which is 1-1/2 inch longer. Years later, a pair of spare axle shafts was located.

The body of the car was built by the Seaman Body Corp., a company noted for having built bodies for some of the great marques. During the tough economic times following World War I, Nash purchased into the W.S. Seaman Co. By the Depression years, most of the bodies built by the Seaman Body Corp. arm of the W.S. Seaman Co. were built for Nash.

The Seaman Body Corp.-built convertible sedan body on Maken's Nash sports dual side-mount tires, five louvers on each side of the hood and a graceful beaver tail-shaped rear body. The front of the car sports a plentitude of chrome, which plates the two Stabilite headlamp buckets, headlamp bar, grille, bumper, two accessory Trippe lamps and flying bird radiator mascot.

Maken was extremely fortunate in obtaining the rare flying bird radiator cap ornament. Something appeared on the Internet from a lady whose father had owned a 1932-'33 Nash and loved the car. Both the father and the car were gone, but he had saved the radiator mascot. Maken bought it and had it replicated in chrome-plated bronze using the lost-wax process. The replica rides on the car and the original remains safely in his collection. It turned out that the mascot was an aftermarket Nash option, and so far, no other original surviving examples have surfaced. It is a one-of-a-kind mascot on a one-of-a-kind car.

Despite that fact that the car is right-hand drive, most of the engine parts are interchangeable with a left-hand-drive model. Of course, the steering column and the steering linkage are unique to the right-hand-drive model. The throttle linkage, the transmission shift stalk and a number of other parts are specific to the right-hand-drive model and replacement parts had to be fabricated.

A league of its own

From today's perspective, Nash did some unusual and strange things. The brakes are four-wheel Steeldraulic units, an excellent system of mechanical brakes used on Hupmobile, Auburn, Pontiac and a few other marques of the era. But the emergency brake is a strange configuration. The e-brake lever did *not* operate a separate brake system; it merely applied the service brakes by hand rather than by foot-pedal.

A search of Nash club records has turned up only two other surviving five-passenger convertible sedan 1073 models, both left-hand drive. But this car remains a one-of-a-kind car that manages to attract attention wherever and whenever it is out on the road.

The restoration of this unique motorcar was orchestrated by the owner, Neil Maken, editor of "Skinned Knuckles" magazine. Contact Skinned Knuckles at P.O. Box 6983, Huntington Beach, CA 92615, by phone at 714-963-1558 or by e-mail at sk.publishing@yahoo.com.

COZY & CLASSY

1932 Pierce-Arrow Model 54 coupe was big on style and looks, but small on passenger space

Joe Cyr's beautiful and durable 1932 Pierce-Arrow Model 54 coupe has had little work done to it since he purchased the car more than 20 years ago.

Somehow, Pierce-Arrow managed to lose $3 million in 1932, and the following year the company was sold to a new group of investors. Six years later, in the summer of 1938, the revered automaker went belly-up. But it seems hard to imagine that the company could have been struggling so mightily in the 1930s, even with the Depression gripping the country, when it was producing vehicles as nice as Joe Cyr's 1932 Model 54 coupe.

Cyr was introduced to the refined and stately Pierce-Arrow at a very young age when his father carted the family around in a 1932 P-A convertible. "That car was basically the same thing as the one I have,

The cozy two-seat interior features an oval-shaped gauge cluster to the right of the driver.

except it was a convertible," noted Cyr, a resident of Old Town, Maine. "He used it go on his honeymoon, and they only had four flat tires!

"We kept it for some time, and I don't remember when it was let go, probably in the late-40s ... I wanted a Pierce-Arrow, and I was looking for a convertible, but convertibles were probably out of my price range. When I saw this one, I went down and drove it and I really liked it."

That purchase occurred back in the mid-1980s, and Cyr has had to do very little to his stunning two-seat closed car since then. He hasn't had it out on the road much in the last few years, instead spending most of his free time behind the wheel of one of his Corvairs, Corvettes or his 1922 Paige, but Cyr admits he is getting the itch to drive the Pierce-Arrow again soon.

"The little that I have driven it on the road, it naturally gets quite a bit of reaction," he said. "There is not too many of

those things sitting around here — a little rural town of 8,000 [people]."

The big news for Pierce-Arrow in 1932 was the addition of two new 12-cylinder models to its menu — the Model 51 and 53. The carryover Model 54 lineup continued to use the 366-cubic inch straight eight that produced 125 hp. The cars also featured front and rear semi-elliptic leaf springs and four-wheel mechanical drum brakes. A three-speed synchromesh transmission was standard, as was "freewheeling" and adjustable "fingertip" hydraulic Delco shocks that could be controlled by a switch on the dash.

The 137-inch-wheelbase lineup included a convertible coupe roadster, five-passenger touring car, phaeton, Brougham, five-passenger sedan, club sedan, club Berlinetta, convertible sedan and Cyr's car, a rumble-seat coupe. Three more Series 54 cars rode on a longer 142-inch wheelbase: a seven-passenger tourer, seven-passenger sedan and a limousine.

The trademark "Archer" hood ornament stands guard on the bow of this Pierce-Arrow.

New body styling for the 1932 model year showed off a rounded roofline and V-shaped radiator shell. New sheet metal made the cars appear longer and sleeker than ever before.

Cyr's coupe is really a small car stretched out on a big-car frame. It features a cozy two-person cockpit flanked by hefty running boards that carry spare tires on both sides. The familiar "Archer" hood ornament adorns the front of the car, while a fold-down luggage rack is anchored to the rear, behind the rumbleseat. Out back is also a unique asymmetrical tail lamp arrangement that has all three round lights mounted horizontally to the left side on a curved stem.

"It's a big, heavy car," Cyr said. "You know it when you go to stop. I don't know what it weighs, to be honest … It rides pretty good, because it has a variable suspension — you can adjust the shocks. It's got the straight eight and it has pretty good pickup, pretty good power.

"I don't know if it's ever been totally restored. I'm not smart enough to tell. The underneath looks to be pretty much original, and I think it might have been repainted probably once. It's still got the good woodwork inside, and there's very little corrosion on it. It wasn't somebody's main car, that's for sure."

Apparently, there weren't enough buyers making the Model 54s their secondary cars, either. Financial hemorrhaging forced Studebaker, which had controlling stock interest in Pierce-Arrow, to sell out to a group in Buffalo, N.Y. The move brought temporary dividends to car lovers in 1933 when the company was able to unveil the legendary Silver Arrow — one of the great automotive designs of any era. The company was on borrowed time, however, and eventually folded in '38, leaving behind a long history of fabulous automobiles, including Cyr's beautiful '32 coupe.

By Angelo Van Bogart

LOAD-BEARING LASALLE
Mysterious and unique pickup is one classy hauler

General Motors did not build LaSalle trucks, but a master builder converted this companion car, originally a 1933 Fisher convertible coupe, into a truck in the fine coachbuilding tradition.

Cars recognized by the Classic Car Club of America are among the hottest types of collector cars, particularly open roadsters and phaetons. These historic cars from what many consider the peak of automobile de-sign are coveted and collected by hobbyists, and their owners often cradle them to the most prestigious concours and club events across the country.

The ultimate sacrilege one could com-

The convertible top is similar to those used on flower cars. This car is too truck-like in appearance to have served as a flower car, although LaSalle touted its cars were "the greatest value offered for funeral service."

mit against this type of car today is modifying it — replacing the straight-eight or V-16 with a small-block Chevy, installing bucket seats in place of finely upholstered bench-type seats or the most offensive crime of all — altering the graceful lines of these often hand-built cars.

Recently, on the showfloor of Jeremy and Dani Thomas' Unique Specialty & Classic Cars in Mankato, Minn. (www.unique-mankato.com), sat a Classic not featured in any LaSalle catalog or coachbuilder's porfolio. The car was a 1933 LaSalle truck, a creation never offered, let alone imagined,

by the automaker. This car, however, defies any modification crimes, and actually serves as a wonderful "should have been" model.

"The first thing people would say is 'I have never seen another one of those,'" said Jeremy Thomas. "We'd say, 'you'll probably never see another one.' That is usually how the conversation started."

Thomas does not know much about the LaSalle's history, since the truck arrived as a trade-in for a 1957 Chevrolet Bel Air convertible he had in stock. The owner trading the LaSalle didn't share much of its history.

The LaSalle truck's builder stamped "Henney" into the tailgate.

"The story on it was he had restored it, and the truck was originally a 1933 LaSalle rumble seat convertible coupe, and we have the documentation from Cadillac verifying this," Thomas said.

The LaSalle was restored with a patina to its paint befitting a workhorse, and since Cadillac and LaSalles of this period are registered by their engine number, the original 115-hp, 353-cid V-8 engine was displayed next to the car for safe keeping. A similar 1933 LaSalle engine was placed under the hood to keep the car-truck hybrid on the road. "The hardest thing for us was trying to put a value on it," Thomas said. "You can't look and see any [comparison sales], so it was a tricky to come up with a value on it. We had to work to put a deal together."

Though they're uncommon, trucks based on Classic cars are not unheard of. Before and after World War II, used medium-size and large cars were sometimes converted to truck duty in order to receive more gas ration stamps during the war, or to give new life to a fine-running car with a damaged rear body. Such trucks were often based on fine cars wearing the names of Lincoln, Packard and Cadillac, and even a few Duesenbergs, among others, since their engines packed the power to haul goods and tow wrecks. Such conversions were typically backyard jobs undertaken with a handsaw or a torch and the finished products often reflected the skills (or lack thereof) of their creators.

A few well-finished vehicles did emerge from such transformations, although they were a rarity. Of those better conversions, this 1933 LaSalle truck is probably among the best in several regards. Not only does the elegant pickup look as though it were a factory job, it may have been completed in the manner that most hand-built Classic cars were constructed — by a coachbuilder.

This 1933 LaSalle began life as a handsome and desirable Fisher-bodied convertible coupe model with a rumble seat, according to Cadillac records. The Cadillac research center determined the car was the sixth of only 146 convertible coupes fitted on LaSalle 345-C chassis that deep Depression year, and was a special-order delivered to the New York branch on Dec. 30, 1932.

How long the car remained in its original configuration is unknown. Somewhere in its history, the car underwent the conversion into a truck in the hands of qualified professionals, possibly following an accident to the rear of its body. It's even possible, though maybe not probable, that the car was specifically ordered for the purpose

The door panels originally featured special-order dove gray cloth, but at some point, beautiful and more utilitarian wood replaced the cloth. It also now features a 1960s-era Ford power steering setup.

of becoming a truck, and the convertible coupe was ordered for its roadster-style windshield frame and cowl design, which it still retains. If this was the case, the builder wisely chose the convertible coupe model, as it was the least expensive open LaSalle at $2,394.

Regardless of what path took it to a professional car builder, the LaSalle convertible coupe's rear body was removed just behind the doors. In this area behind the front seat, the body was finished in the shape of a typical truck cab's rear and a truck bed was fitted atop the rear of the chassis. To cover the passenger compartment, a collapsible roadster-style top was placed over the seats, though it had a different design than the original LaSalle top. In back, the LaSalle truck received a tailgate with the name of Henney (a coachbuilder) emblazoned across it, as well as a trailer hitch.

The service for which the LaSalle was intended to perform has been lost to time. The truck could easily have been planned as a flower car-type vehicle, which was just coming into vogue in the 1930s. Many flower cars, especially early flower cars used for hauling floral memorials, featured a convertible-shape roof very much like this LaSalle's top.

Without factory records or those of a coachbuilder, it's impossible to date the work on the LaSalle or determine its original purpose, if it was built in this configuration when it was a new or slightly used vehicle. The Fall 1978 issue of The Professional Car includes a transcript from a speech given by H. Reid Horner, the director of personnel at Henney from 1928-'54.

In his interview, Horner noted that flower cars were built by Henney in batches of 10 at a time and were special-orders. Before the company began exclusively building bodies on new Packard chassis in 1937, Henney built bodies on Buick, Auburn, Pierce-Arrow, Reo, Pontiac and Oldsmobile chassis. He said bodies were built on other makes, including LaSalle, on a customer's special order. With this window, it's possible that Thomas' LaSalle was built some time before 1937, regardless of what type of service its owner intended.

Unfortunately, Horner's speech does not mention a LaSalle truck, leaving the nature of this truck open to conjecture. If the LaSalle was not built as a flower car, it's possible that it served as an in-plant hauler for a business or for a Cadillac and LaSalle dealer. It's also possible that a LaSalle lover with taste simply wanted the utility of a truck and the panache of a LaSalle for business or personal use.

Today, many enthusiasts would consider it a criminal act to turn a Classic into a truck. However, restoring this unique LaSalle back into a convertible coupe would be equally punishable if it were truly a rare reminder of a once-common conversion, and if it has spent most of its life as a coachbuilt truck, not a convertible coupe. Luckily, Texan truck and Classic car collector Richard Mitchell, the new owner of this Henney LaSalle, has no plans to rewrite the LaSalle's history again.

Editor's note: After this story was originally published, Old Cars Weekly *readers confirmed this LaSalle was recently converted into a truck in the style of a 1930s conversion.*

DEPRESSION FIGHTERS

Hard times had Studebaker down, but not out

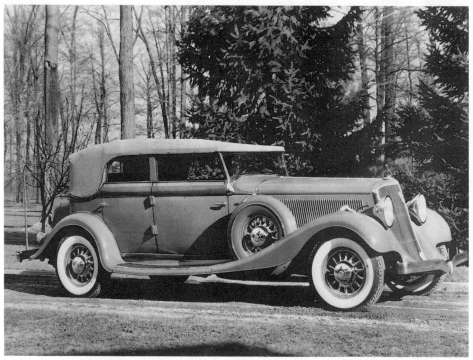

1933 Studebaker Model 92 Speedway State Convertible Sedan

The year 1933 found the automobile industry in the depths of the Great Depression. The worsening economy hit all automakers hard, but it was the independents that suffered the most. Pierce-Arrow, Auburn and Duesenberg as well as many others, all stopped production during the 1930s. 1935 was a dismal year for Studebaker, too, but the firm survived even as production plummeted. Internal restructuring of model lines brought the prestige of the President nameplate to a lower price level that, while still a couple of steps above Ford and Chevrolet in quality and price, gave astute buyers more value for their dollars.

Two President Eight series were offered for 1933. The 82 models were the smaller

1933 Studebaker President Regal Roadster

and less powerful of the two lines; virtually identical in size, performance and features to the 1932 Commander. The Model 92, called the President Speedway Eight, was the larger and more powerful with its wheelbase of 135 inches and proven 336.7-cubic inch inline eight-cylinder engine.

Styling features of the 82 included a more radically slanted V-type radiator grille, skirted fenders, double inside sun visors and beaver tail rear styling. Standard equipment included a Stromberg carburetor, Delco Remy ignition, Bendix vacuum-boosted power brakes, automatic choke, automatic starter, automatic manifold heat control, downdraft carburetion, ball bearing spring shackles, free-wheeling and a 17 1/2-gallon fuel tank.

Despite the economic stress of the time, Studebaker initially offered some 41 model/body style combinations for 18933. Twelve of the these were eventually dropped with the temporary discontinuance of the Dictator series. The President Eight accounted for eight of these combinations with prices ranging from $1,325 for a two-door cope,

Above, 1933 Studebaker Model 92 State Limousine
Below, 1933 Studebaker President Eight Convertible Coupe

1933 Studebaker Regal St. Regis Brougham

1933 Studebaker Commander Eight Model 73 Coupe

to $1,650 for a five-passenger convertible sedan.

Model year production topped out at 45,074 vehicles for all of Studebaker's 1933 lines, but on March 18, 1933, the company went into receivership, a temporary embarrassment from which it would quickly emerge.

By John Wesley Gilmore

REJECTED THEN, CHERISHED NOW

Once considered an ugly duckling, this 1934 Auburn phaeton is an attention magnet

John Wesley Gilmore fell in love with this 1934 Auburn phaeton in the early 1960s, when it was owned by a friend. Nearly 50 years later, the car joined Gilmore's garage and then underwent substantial work to make it drivable again.

Dejection, disappointment and downright gloom must have been overwhelming as the leadership of the Auburn Automobile Co. — Hubert Beal, Lou Manning and Harold Ames — made their way back from New York after unveiling their new sleek, raked-back design for 1934. Auburn was firmly entrenched among the top marques and the entirely new streamlined look, perfected by stylist Alan Leamy, was designed to pull the company through the Great Depression.

However, that was not to be. Reception to the design was negative, with dealers

and potential purchasers alike giving it the "thumbs down" and calling for a new design. It is said that before they arrived back in Auburn, Ind., they had made the decision to cut the 1934-style production back and launch a new model as quickly as possible. The 1935 Auburns were introduced in September 1934.

E. L. Cord had taken over the Auburn Automobile Co. in 1924 and became the genius to elevate the Auburn automobiles to an elite status. His success led him to buy Dusenberg in 1926, Columbia Axle Co. and Lycoming Engine Co. in 1927 and the Stinson Aircraft Co. in 1929, the same year

L-29 Cord was launched. He bought airlines and other manufacturing companies as his empire grew, but Auburn remained the cornerstone of his empire and was undoubtedly among the most profitable.

By 1934, E.L. Cord had moved his family to England in order to protect his children from criminal threats, and his interest and oversight of the Auburn Co. was said to be virtually non-existent.

Although some other automobile manufacturers had previously built all-steel vehicles with hydraulic brakes, 1934 was the first year for Auburn. Competition during the Depression years was extreme and

Auburn's 1934 models were designed for survival in that crowded field. However, Auburn did not stray far from its initial high-quality components; all-leather upholstery, massive chrome inside and out, Columbia two-speed rear end and lots of high-end features made it difficult to produce a profit. As an example, the 652-Y phaeton with all those features sold for only $945 in order to

compete with Ford, Chevrolet and other popular makes. Even though new models were developed for 1935 and 1936, the Auburn was unable to attract enough customers to survive and the last cars rolled out of the plant in 1937.

An ignored Auburn gets attention

My wife thinks I am a bit demented, or even more than a bit. Most of her lady friends agree. But the majority of guys will recognize the raw, blinding emotion when a very special automobile crosses your path. Burning desire and passion does not properly describe the forces at work here,

and worse yet, sometimes it never happens. I've been fortunate that such an occurrence has happened to me more times than I want to admit.

The first instant infatuation came in the early 1960s when my new friend Al Clark opened his garage door to give me a peek at his 1934 Auburn phaeton. The sight of his beautiful car struck me hard, but this maroon lovely could not possibly be bought. Al had purchased the car in Seaside, Ore., in 1941, coughing up the extravagant sum of $260 — $200 down and two monthly payments of $30 each. By this time, he had already cherished it for more than 20 years.

Over the next 20 years, I had many opportunities to enjoy the Auburn, but all the time knowing it would never be mine.

In the late 1980s, Al retired and he and his wife departed Edmonds, Wash., for the warm dry climate of California and the Auburn went with them. I kissed the car goodbye forever.

In the following years, my wife and I participated in the annual 200-mile endurance run in Santa Clara, Calif., with our 1925 Model T Ford speedster. On arrival in Santa Clara, Al, whose profession was a mechanic, would greet us with tools in hand to help prepare the speedster for the grueling event, and he always brought the Auburn for me to enjoy.

Regrettably, Al's wife, Marion, passed away and, soon after, Al had a massive stroke and died. Again, I thought about the Auburn, but felt uncomfortable asking his daughters if the car might be for sale. So, once again, believing the car would be sold in California, I kissed the Auburn goodbye.

Unbeknownst to me, Al's daughters had the car transported back to the Seattle area and placed in a storage unit. Nearly two years later, Al's daughter called me and asked if I would help her move the Auburn to her home in Everett. We were able to get it started, and it limped to her garage with only minor braking ability and firing on three or four cylinders. She was going to save the car for her grandson. The car would sit in her garage, uncovered and untouched, for the next 18 years.

A year ago, we received a Christmas card from Al's daughter and she asked, "Do you know anyone who might be interested in buying my dad's old Auburn?" After my wife scraped me off the ceiling, that early day emotion returned with a vengeance and I will resist telling the world of my childish response. The decision in recent years to avoid another restoration project, albeit not a full one, quickly evaporated and I purchased the car. It was complete, had never had any rust, and was generally in what I considered to be a solid condition.

Reviving the Auburn after 20 years

Knowing the great condition of the Auburn in past years and how pampered it had been, I concluded that it would be relatively easy to get it back in shape. Wrong!

Although the car had always been garaged, the area was unheated and the damage caused by all those years of inactivity was beyond my imagination. Some things survived. A professional detailing of the paint proved reasonably successful and, since the car had been placed on blocks, the tires remained like new.

Although the car was out of the sunlight, being exposed to moisture for all those years meant the bright work had tarnished to the point that virtually all of it required re-chroming. Some of the upholstery was original and now worn be-

yond use. The once-black top had become a sickly tan, was generally shabby and had to be replaced.

Many of the mechanical parts were deteriorated beyond repair. The gas tank was so corroded that a simple flush would not suffice; it had to be dismantled, sandblasted and welded back together. Of course, the gas lines had to be cleaned out and the carburetor was plugged beyond belief.

The brakes were absolutely useless. The master cylinder and all the wheel cylinders were seized solid and all the lines were so deteriorated that total replacement was necessary. Fortunately, the radiator and engine had antifreeze in them and only required several flushings and minor repair. More than 70 years of wear and tear caused the wiring to be frayed and potentially dangerous, which made a new harness essential.

The engine had been rebuilt before Al retired, and after some cleaning and praying, it purred like a kitten. The transmission and two-speed rear end had grease build up that was hard as a rock, but when thoroughly cleaned, everything proved to be in excellent condition.

Now that most of the work has been completed, I can report that it is an outstanding tour car. With the two-speed rear end, it travels with the big boys on the highways at a comfortable speed of 55 to 60 mph, handles like a new car and attracts lots of attention, due to the fact that most people have never seen one.

Although it was once rejected, today the 1934 Auburn custom phaeton is highly cherished and perhaps the rarest of all Classic-era Auburns. Exact manufacturing numbers have long since disappeared, but Auburn Cord Duesenberg Automobile Museum officials say that, "With a little 'creative' calculation, we could estimate that Auburn built around 160 1934 652-Y phaetons." How many of the phaetons came from the factory with the Columbia two-speed rear end and a trunk, such as my car has, is unknown. However, at one point, ACD officials said "There are probably no more than six 652-Y phaetons with trunks remaining."

I think my old friend Al Clark would be pleased to know that the Auburn is getting lots of attention and will continue to be highly cherished.

Story by Peter Winnewisser
Photos by Jason Tagliaferri

YOU'RE NEVER TOO YOUNG FOR A '34 FORD

The 1934 Ford Cabriolet — this one owned by Jason Tagliaferri of Gloversville, N.Y. — is, arguably, the best looking of the 1934 V-8 passenger cars. Tagliaferri's unrestored car has dual horns, dual cowl lights, dual bumper guards and the V-8 emblem. (Peter Winnewisser photo)

The 1934 Fords celebrate their 75th anniversary this year. According to the Ford Motor Co. World Production Report, 563,921 Ford passenger cars rolled off the assembly lines that year. Thousands of them are still in the hands of collectors today, but few are as authentic, even to the original paint in showroom condition, as the 1934 Cabriolet (model 40, type 760) owned by 33-year-old Jason Tagliaferri of Gloversville, N.Y.

Tagliaferri is both a perceptive and patient young man. Perceptive, because he can appreciate the charisma and historical

The car is parked in front of the building in which it was stored for more than 40 years.

significance of an authentic and original Ford, even though he is, at heart, a street rod man with a particular love for the Deuce and his 1950 Mercury. Patient, because he spent 10 years of watchful waiting before he was able to make the Cabriolet his own. Here's the story.

The car was assembled in early May of 1934, one of 14,496 produced that year. The factory price was $590. It was sold by Maylender-Hughes dealership in Gloversville, N.Y., to the first owner in late 1934 and then sold two or three months later, in early 1935, to Henry Born Sr. Born drove the car to church and work. He washed and waxed it every Sunday after church. According to the service records, the car was

rarely driven in the winter months. In the early 1940s it was stored in a garage with about 72,000 miles on the odometer.

The Cabriolet rested in the garage until the mid '80s, when Henry Born Jr., who inherited the car after his father's passing, took it out of storage, rebuilt the engine and brakes and installed a new convertible top and five new tires. He then drove the car sparingly, putting about 2,400 miles on it over 20-plus years.

Tagliaferri and Born met because they stored their cars in the same building. They became friends, kept in touch over a 10-year period during which Tagliaferri, who greatly admired the '34, from time to time expressed his interest in buying the

**The dual horns, dual cowl lights, dual bumper guards and the
V-8 emblem all decorate the front end.**

car. In October 2007, that hope became a reality.

Since buying the Ford, Tagliaferri has driven it more than 2,000 miles. "I enjoy it very much, it is a piece of history," he said. Last fall, he entered it in the Historic Preservation of Original Features category at the AACA meet in Hershey and won an award. He has the license plates that were on the car when it was sold by the dealer, numerous service records of work done on the car in the early years, the original owner's manual and the installation instructions for the aftermarket Philco radio in the car. In the future, he hopes to replace the new top with the original one, which was taken off only because of a leak. He also has the original boot for the top.

One of the prime features of the car that immediately captures attention is the mostly original Vineyard Green body and wheel color. The paint condition is spectacular. Possibly, the frequent waxing in the early years helped to preserve it. Except for some paint work on the left front fender in the late 1930s or early '40s due to a minor accident, and the paint on the spare tire cover, the paint on the car is as it came from the factory. The striping, including the stripes on the hood louvers, is also from the factory.

The upholstery is the original leather

The interior features leather upholstery and original floor mats.

and leatherette installed at the factory in both the interior and the rumble seat. The floor mats are also original and in decent condition. The dash has been repainted. The chrome is original. The car currently rides on whitewall tires, but they will eventually be switched to blackwalls. The V-8 powerplant was installed at the factory. It does have 1936 water pumps and the incorrect fuel pump. These will be returned to the factory-installed units, which are in the owner's possession.

Typical of the DeLuxe cars, the Cabriolet has dual horns, cowl lamps, tail lamps, and a chrome-plated windshield frame. The interior has an adjustable seat, cigar lighter, ash tray and glove box. The operating handle for the rumble seat is located behind the passenger side of the front seat. In addition to the radio, accessories include the metal spare tire cover, spare tire lock, bumper guards and the original greyhound grille ornament.

Tagliaferri operates Tag's Upholstery in Gloversville, N.Y., specializing in custom auto, home and boat upholstery. He has restored several cars, including a 1966 Mustang with custom upholstery for his mother. He also helped his father restore a 1957 Ford retractable, which has won several national awards, including Junior and Senior Awards at AACA meets. About 10 years ago, he built a 1932 Ford three-window coupe from scratch for his brother. Currently, he is working on a 1932 Ford five-window coupe for himself. It will have a stock-looking body, a 302 Ford engine, automatic overdrive and four-wheel independent suspension.

Tagliaferri's first love, however, is his 1950 Mercury, which he has owned since he was 14. "I learned how to weld as I chopped the top on the car when I was 16," he says. "It is now a full custom. I decided a long time ago that I would never sell the Merc, because I've talked to a lot of guys my dad's age or older and they all say the same thing: 'I wish I still had my first car, I never should have sold it.' The Merc is my first car, and I hope I will be able to continue to say that I own it for a long time."

So there you have the story. A young man who is especially fond of his custom Merc and '32 Ford street rod. He is just 33 years old, with a world of old car experience. He specializes in upholstery work and also has an appreciation for the historical charm of his pristine '34 Ford Cabriolet. It's not just the older generation that has a love for vintage iron.

By Brian Earnest

FORTUNATE FORD

1934 Ford sedan delivery survived the 9-5 toils to become rare show piece

Left, Darrell and Lela Sago's rare 1934 Ford sedan delivery has undergone a meticulous restoration and is now one of the finest remaining examples of the breed.

Right, The Briggs-built '34 sedan delivery body was longer than the standard Tudor, used Fordor front doors and featured a 36-inch-wide by 34-inch-high rear door.

Cross-over vehicles have certainly been all the rage on the new car front in recent years. Every domestic car maker has been working overtime to come out with vehicles that seem to blur the lines between sedan, station wagon, SUV and truck. The "tweener" certainly seems like the car of the future.

But a look back through history shows that crossover vehicles that melded the best traits of cars and trucks and SUVs are certainly nothing new. Even back before World War II, automakers, including Ford Motor Co., were offering such amalgamations they called "sedan deliveries." The moniker is sometimes confused with the more popular "panel deliveries" of the period, but there was a major difference between

the two: The sedan deliveries were built on a car chassis, while the panel deliveries were classified as trucks because they rode on truck chassis.

Often, sedan deliveries were basically sedans converted into delivery cars. In 1932, Ford sedan deliveries featured Tudor bodies with blanked-out rear windows and a rear-opening door, but in 1933, Ford sedan delivery bodies were more than just converted Tudors; the Briggs-built sedan delivery body was longer than the standard Tudor, used Fordor front doors and featured a 36-inch-wide x 34-inch-high rear door. The spare tire was carried in a front fender well.

For 1934, the year of the featured vehicle, sedan deliveries were little changed

from 1933 and continued to be available in both four-cylinder and flathead V-8 versions, and a total of 9,021 were built. It's anybody's guess how many are left, but they seem to be about as common these days as wolly mammoths. And it's a fair bet you'll never see a 1934 sedan delivery nicer than the near-perfect rig owned by Darrell and Lela Sago of Festus, Mo.

Despite the remarkable condition of the Sagos' sedan delivery, it might not turns heads when it makes a rare appearance at a show due to its muted black-and-brown color scheme. But for those who appreciate the beauty of

a finely restored V-8 Ford, and a rare model at that, this squeaky clean sedan delivery is a true treasure.

"There really aren't many of them around," Darrell Sago said. "I know of about six of them around the country. "This one's a national show winner. It's been gone over pretty good. It's pretty amazing, really."

Sago owns a 1940 Ford and says he's had "10 or 12" old Ford pickups over the years, but he took on a new challenge about seven years ago when he bought the panel delivery from a man in California. The car was not finished, but a lot of the heavy lifting had already been done in its restoration by the time he purchased it.

According to the Lagos, the car was brought back to showroom condition by noted restorer Don Thelan. Much of the original sheet metal is still intact. The interior has been upgraded with a Deluxe dash, cigar lighter, visors and wood grain on the dash and window moldings. Upholstery is all vinyl, and was done by a former member of Boyd Coddington's shop. The wood in the cargo area floor was re-done by Doug Car of The Wood N Car in Signal Hill, Calif.

"When I bought it, it was in fairly decent shape," Sago said. "I had to re-do the fenders on it … Now, it is straight as an arrow, I'll tell you. There's no putty or anything on it. Not a wrinkle on it. It's 100 percent, and underneath it's a shiny as it is on top. It's so shiny underneath that it looks like its powdercoated."

The 1934 Model 40 V-8 sedan deliveries had only mild styling revisions to distinguish them from the previous 1933 models. Like all Ford passenger cars, the 1934 grille was slightly changed, the hood louvers of all 1934 models were now straight, and the Ford script on the grille shell was revised. The engine received a new fuel induction system with counter-balanced cast alloy steel crankshafts, open skirt pistons, water-line thermostats, improved fuel pump and unitized valve assemblies. The cargo area was 59 inches long and 45-3/4 inches wide with insulating board side panels. There was a single bucket seat, one sun visor and a three-speed floor shifted manual transmission. Deluxe models had pinstriping, cowl lights, twin horns and two tail lamps.

Everything is present and accounted for on the Sagos' Ford – and in perfect working order.

"We had to re-do the engine — actually, I had to do it twice, because it wasn't done right the first time … I've had to change probably 99 percent of all nuts and screws on it. It's got new tires on it, new battery … I did a lot of work on it, really."

"The running gear underneath it, trans-mission and rear, that's the same as on the car … It's small, it's not very big. I've run into a lot of problems with it, but I think I've fixed everything."

That work has been noticed in recent years at two noteworthy shows. In 2005, the car received 954 points of a possible 1,000 at a show in Keystone, Colo. "It had 46 points deducted, and 20 of those were for hydraulic brakes, which are for safe-ty," Sago said. "Then it won the Dearborn Award in 2008," when it received a score of 967, including another 20-point deduction for the brakes.

But the beautiful Ford's appearances in public are few and far between these days, as are its trips out of the Sagos' driveway. "I mostly keep it stuck in the garage. I'm just afraid to drive it and devalue it," Darrell admitted. "It's so nice, I just don't want to drive the dang thing. It's pathetic, really. I do feel guilty, and I'd feel guilty if I drove it and devalued it."

It might be a bit of an unlikely show pony, given that it was born to be a work-ing vehicle, but the Lagos' Show-Me State '34 sedan delivery is rare, meticulously re-stored, and pretty darn cool.

THE TEST OF MILES

Louis Chevrolet and Sun Oil proved the value of new oils with the '35 Chevrolet

Above, as Louis Chevrolet proved, a 1935 Chevrolet coach could run with 20W oil in the winter without negative results. He made his point in a 5,000-mile run. Below, knee-Action Ride on the 1935 Chevrolet was touted by a handful of specially made units with the mechanism lifted high for all to see in operation.

It wasn't easy being Chevrolet in 1935. Its papa, General Motors, set high goals for the division. Like most children, Chevrolet would have to work its way there, using every bit of muscle to claim and hold top post as the nation's family-budget sales leader.

What did the brand offer? Two series: Standard (Series EC with 107-inch wheelbase) and Master Deluxe (Series ED/EA with 113-inch platform). Both ran the respected inline six with cast-iron block, three main bearings and overhead valves, as customers had come to expect when the engine bowed for 1929. Displacement was 206.8 cubic inches with braking horsepower of 74 at 3,200 rpm.

To please Daddy, Chevrolet rolled out five Standard models (sport roadster, phaeton, coupe, coach and sedan), while the Master Deluxe carried six (coupe, coach and sedan, plus sport coupe, sport sedan and town sedan). Standards ranged in price from $465 to $550, while Master Deluxes stepped up from $560 to $675. Not much difference in dollar spread by today's standards, but the difference was about 17-19 percent for the more well-endowed Master Deluxe.

In Master Deluxe guise, the 1935 Chevrolet offered Knee-Action Ride, a novel system for cushioning body jostle over rough roads. To promote the innovation, special demonstrator versions were made for public relations. The models had their front fenders cut back to allow extensions from the front suspension. Metal arms extended as high as the hood, with Knee-Action units atop. This allowed bystander, rider and driver the opportunity to watch how the mechanism worked.

Master Deluxe Chevrolets for 1935 also offered another improvement: Turret-top construction, advertised as steel protection for safety. Lesser offerings in the Chevrolet line had the composite top of old, still fine and usable, but not as marketable as all-steel tops. It was an era on the verge of all-steel bodies across the industry. But not yet.

Innovations. Good pricing. Wonderful dealer network. GM was proud of Chevy's success. But the parent also knew that any make of car is only as good as the current model. Reputations have been won or lost in a single sales year. So Chevrolet officials set out to put their favorite car front and center in the public eye.

It remains to be shown who it was that had the idea of taking a Chevrolet across country in late 1934 to prove the worth of light-weight engine oil. The car chosen by AAA to run the test was a Chevrolet two-door coach. The driver, of all people, was Louis Chevrolet, the famous race car driver who allowed his name and reputation to become a household fixture on GM's favorite low-priced car.

A stunt? Hardly. A practical exposé? Probably. Good for Chevrolet? Let the results speak.

First, the crankcase was sealed. No oil could be added. The point was to show the enduring properties of thinner oil, since "automobile dealers and garage men, in common with automobile owners, have long regarded thickness as one of the prime measures of an oil's lubricating quality, as well as its ability to 'stand up' under heavy service," said a reporter assigned to the drill. The test came on the heels of the introduction of winter-weight motor oil in 1933. Manufacturers were ready to push the idea of 10W and 20W oils as safe.

So it was that Sun Oil Co. sponsored the event in November of 1934 as the new '35 Chevrolets were heading toward showrooms.

AAA supervised the test.

"The test was enough of a 'stunt' to arrest public attention, yet it was so rigidly supervised as to make its outcome thoroughly authenticated," it was noted. To make that happen, AAA observer H.H. Allen rode with Mr. Chevrolet. Sun Oil provided a photographer, but that was all. Of course, the Chevrolet motor car was the star at each stop, and the glamour of Mr. Chevrolet still rubbed off favorably onto the marque.

Average speed for the six-cylinder car was 42 mph. Preparation was made to assure no loss of oil from the engine due to gasket leakage or other means. Sunoco 20W oil was used. One little twist was added: special piston rings were installed (two No. 70, one No. 80 Perfect Circle brand). A new breather was installed, and the oil pan had a reinforced flange.

Louis Chevrolet left on Nov. 6. His trip took him through Norwood and Pittsburgh, Pa.; Canton, Ohio; Fort Wayne, Ind.; Detroit; Indianapolis; then to Miami through the Everglades, and back to Norwood. He registered 5,009.6 miles in 119 hours, 31 minutes. Gasoline consumption was 267.25 gallons (18.75 miles per gallon). No breakdowns or malfunctions marred the trip, which spoke well of the Chevrolet.

Of the 5.15 quarts of 20W engine oil in the motor, 1.46 quarts remained — "enough oil…for several hundred miles more, and the drained oil contained only fifteen-hundredths of one percent dirt and sludge. Oil consumption was 3.68 quarts, which is at the rate of 1,360 miles to the quart," it was reported.

After the run, AAA tore down the engine. According to Mr. Chevrolet and AAA's Mr. Allen, the bearings, pistons and rings were still in "first-class condition." The wear was hardly measurable on the new car.

It was noted that "Mr. Chevrolet considers this test to be more exacting than speedway tests, because it involves maximum speeds considerably greater than the average speed." To maintain the average speed above 40 mph for the entire trip, Mr. Chevrolet drove long stretches at 50 mph. His conclusion: lightweight oil was fine for winter use and provided "perfect lubrication." He even concluded that 20W oil could be used in climates that were moderately warm, as was the case with his southern swing.

The race car legend further concluded that the 20W oil was fine for speeds below 50, but above that mark there were higher operating temperatures that stressed the oil's properties. A heavier oil for those severe conditions was suggested.

Said Chevrolet: "This test has proved to me that the recommendation of car manufacturers to use 20W oil for temperatures averaging as low as zero is the best contribution that has been made to the right kind of lubrication in winter, because undoubtedly, this oil will let motorists start much quicker and will give them 100 percent lubrication… something that motorists believed could not be done with such a light oil."

And a new Chevrolet was at the heart of the test, making its General Motors parent proud.

By Brian Earnest

FAMILY AIR-LOOM

Treasured '35 Ford has a long history of hidden high-flying gadgetry

Bill Burns of Brownsville, Texas, spent many years slowly restoring his father's unique 1935 Ford Deluxe Tudor. The car features many pieces of airplane gadetry, which were inspired by Gilford Burns' job repairing aircraft instruments during World War II.

Bill Burns chuckles a bit when he thinks back to his father Gilford's "tinkering" tendencies. In some ways, the senior Burns was a bit of a closet customizer, adding unique and subtle details that certainly weren't "factory issue" to his stately, buttoned-down 1935 Ford Deluxe Tudor.

Bill just figures his old man loved his gray Ford so much, he couldn't resist giving it a few tweeks and do-dads that made it different from any other car on the road.

Either way, the unique old Ford has been a beloved member of the family since the day Bill's dad got it new as a going-off-to-college gift 73 years ago. The elder Burns died 48 years ago, but thanks to his son's undying affection for the car, the venerable Ford has never looked better — well, at least not for a long time.

"The car was originally purchased by my dad — given to him new when he went to college," recalled Burns, a resident of

Among the car's more obvious modifications were its aircraft-issue lamps, mounted above the bumper, that "lit up the countryside," according to Bill Burns.

Brownsville, Texas. "It was his personal vehicle his entire life, and he died in '61. He and my mom dated in the car. My brother and I dated in the car … The car has quite a family history to it.

"Dave loved that automobile … I mean, he drove it from 1935 to 1961. He loved the car, and that's why we kept it."

One of the reasons Gilford loved his Ford was because of all the fun little things he was able to do to the car, thanks to his fondness for gadgetry and his job as an instrument technician for Pan American Airways. Some old Fords from that era got flames and scallops, some went without fenders or hoods. Gilford Burns' car cruised around with various airplane parts bolted all over it.

"Pan American Airways, during World War II, they had an instrument repair shop, and they sent airplane instruments there to get fixed," Bill said. Gilford ran the shop, and "would occasionally modify some-

thing and put in on the '35 Ford," according to Bill. "Instrumentation, spark plugs, a water injecting system for the carburetor … I could go on and on. It had some rather unique features on it.

"The car didn't need 'em, but he was just dealing with these instruments and he loved that car and just had to put something on it… He had altimeters and, of course, temperature gauges and pressure gauges…"

"He latched onto a couple of aircraft landing lights that were about the size of the fog lights that were on the Deluxe model Fords. Well, we used to travel in Mexico for weeks at a time when I was a kid. If you ever travel down there, you know the roads aren't normal, and if you meet a truck down there on the road, they're not gonna dim (their high-beams). Well, man, I'll tell you, those lights lit up the countryside. Those truck drivers would be hustling to get their lights dimmed."

Most of the changes of the aeronautical variety were cosmetic, but not all of them. Bill found out the hard way it was best to be careful with the oversized airplane spark plugs his dad decided to use as an experiment. "Those spark plugs were really long — they probably stuck up twice as high as regular plugs," he said. "That car had one whale of a spark, I wanna tell you. I was helping him one night in the garage and I bumped into one of those things, and it knocked me halfway across the floor!"

Oversized plugs and headlights that you could see from space were clearly not standard equipment on the 1935 Deluxes, but the mildly restyled Fords did have their share of accessories and refinements that year.

Ford claimed "Greater Beauty, Greater Comfort, and Greater Safety" for 1935. The narrower radiator grille lost its sharply veed base and four horizontal bars helped accentuate the 1935 model's new lower and more streamlined appearance. The fender outlines were much more rounded and the side hood louvers received three horizontal bright stripes. In profile, the Ford windshield was seen more sharply sloped than previously. The parking lamps became integrated with the headlights and the headlamp shells were painted body color. For the first time, Ford offered a built-in trunk for its Tudor and Fordor models, and all Fords had front-hinged doors front and rear.

Deluxe Fords had a set of horizontal bars running down the center section of the dash. External distinctions included bright wind-shield and grille trim work on the Deluxe models, and dual exposed horns with twin tail lamps in back. A convertible sedan was new, and the Victoria model was discontinued.

The engine was the 221-cid L-head V-8, which produced 85 hp at 3,800 rpm. Alas, the engine in Burns' car was damaged by what Bill termed a "rare freeze" during winter and replaced with a "a late-'30s '85.'"

The cars rode on a 112-inch wheelbase with 6.00 x 16 tires. A sliding-gear, manual-floor-shift transmission was standard on the '35s.

"In the mid to late-'50s, when I was a teenager, I used to drive the car a lot and it had an 85-hp V-8 in it, and I'd drag race that thing," Bill said.

"Of course, Dad would have killed me, but it really got up and went."

Wire wheels could wear optional white-wall tires. Other options included a radio, antenna, heater, cigar lighter, clock, seat covers, spotlight, dual windshield wipers, greyhound radiator ornament, luggage rack and a banjo-type steering wheel.

Ford was the nation's top-selling car maker for 1935 and offered five different Standard body styles and 10 different Deluxe models. The Burns' car was one of 87,336 of the Tudor trunk sedans built, making it the third-most popular car in the 15-car lineup.

When Bill got the car following his father's passing, he knew he'd eventually give it a loving and well-deserved restoration, but

the process wound up taking longer than he planned. "I took it down basically to the frame and I started over with it, but I got transferred for my job every two or three years and it took a long time to get the thing finished up... I've lived in various places around the country. We moved a lot, and all these companies I went to work for, my main stipulation was, 'If you want me, then the car is coming, too.' For so long, the car was in various stages of restoration during all these moves. There was probably more money spent on it moving than the car was ever worth."

Bill finally finished his restoration in early 1980s, preserving as many of his father's airplane modifications as he could.

The transmission and rear end are original. The underside and body panels were sand blasted and painted with zinc chromate and black paint.

Fittingly, the car wound up on display for a number of years in the Confederate Air Force Museum in Brownsville before the family took it back seven or eight years ago — still with only 74,000 miles on the odometer.

Bill has now turned over the keys to the family heirloom Ford to his own son, Greg, who is storing it in southeast Arizona. At this point in the car's life, it wouldn't seem right for it to ever leave the family.

"I restored it because of the love my father had for it," Bill says. "And it got me started in antique cars. I've had two Corvettes and T-bird and few other things ... I've had my toys, and this car was his toy."

By John R. Ferullo

SERIOUS SERIES 60
After a long restoration, a '36 Cadillac comes to life

Almost all old cars have a story. My story is on the history of my 1936 Cadillac's origins, restoration and its present-day condition.

I own and operate two property and casualty insurance agencies, and in the selling process, my staff and I visit many businesses and homes. One of the businesses I visited back in 1992 was S&B Auto Body, located in the borough of West Chester in Pennsylvania. The owner was Samuel Bal-sama. He was an older gentleman who had spent his career in the collision business. He turned his business into a father-and-son team after his son, Peter, expressed his interest in the collision industry. The first time I entered the shop, I noted a half-assembled Packard and a tan 1936 Cadillac Series 60 coupe covered with dust. I had to ask about the cars, especially the Cadillac.

Sam and Peter explained to me that the Cadillac was purchased from General

Sales, which was a local Cadillac agency in the borough of West Chester. After 72 years, General Sales still exists, although under different ownership. I researched the car's history through the GM Heritage Center, and it provided me with a book on 1936 Cadillacs, which included a wealth of information. It also supplied a copy of the original shipping receipt, which showed the order date of Aug. 12, 1935, and the car's VIN. The car was owned by Mr. and Mrs. Smitson, who lived on a farm in Chester County, Pa. Peter Balsama recalled the couple added a spare gas tank and took the Cadillac down to New Mexico and back. After Mr. Smitson died, the car spent a lot

of time in their barn.

Since Samuel Balsama did work for General Sales, a service manager from the agency told Samuel about the car as they provided service on the Cadillac, and he purchased the car. The car was a 25-footer painted tan over the original black color. The Caddy remained in the Balsama family with Peter retaining ownership. Each year, I would visit the shop for the insurance renewal and ask about the Cadillac.

Although Peter had planned to restore the car at some point, he decided to sell it in 2005. I have a 12-year-old son who is also a car enthusiast, so I brought him to see the car and the deal was made. My son

took pictures in the Caddy with Samuel Balsama.

The restoration

I spent 15 years in the collision business and I worked for a family-owned garage in Philadelphia where I received hands-on experience in auto body and fender work. I water-sanded the paint, then machine-polished it alone with some other minor repairs and realized it was still a 20-footer. The Cadillac did not have any missing parts, and all of the numbers matched, which was important since the 1936 Cadillac Series 60 was a single-model-year car. The decision was made to complete a nut-and-bolt resto-ration. The goal was to restore the Cadillac to its original quality and beauty.

With a project of this size, the car needed a name. Of course, I named the car after my daughter, Sophia.

I searched local facilities to complete the engine rebuilding and body restoration. The engine was sent to Fred's Engine Service in Coatesville, Pa. The body was sent to Precision Auto Restoration in Havertown, Pa.

When Fred first started the engine and ran the transmission, we knew both would need a complete rebuild. This was a painstaking experience, since many parts are not available for this series. Fortunately, Fred

also had a background from his family's machine shop business. He was successful in making or modifying several parts on the engine and transmission. This process took more than six months to complete.

When the body arrived at Precision Auto Restoration, the 20-footer was going to need much more work than anticipated. The nut-and-bolt restoration began. The car was taken apart, the frame was media blasted and every part was attended to. The parts that were not repairable presented the same problems as the engine. A single-

model-year production car of which very few remained in existence presented the need for an extensive search effort. Searching all the trade magazines, Internet and shows to find the needed parts became a nightly activity. In my search, I found the same car posted on the Internet from a show in Michigan. A Google search found the owner, Fred Swan. I called Fred several times with questions about the car, and he was always eager to help. Many parts had to be fabricated to maintain the goal of a show-quality restoration. The estimated

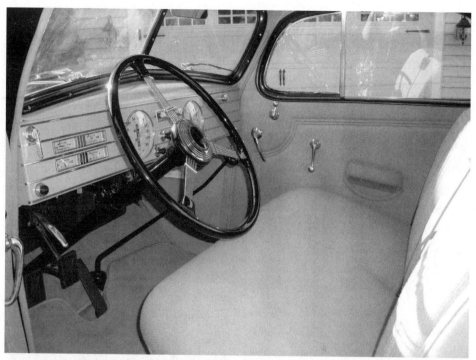

one-year restoration of the body turned into a two-year affair.

The interior of the car had seat covers. When the seat covers were removed, it was revealed that the original interior was intact. Futureline Auto Tops in Exton, Pa., handled the interior restoration. Mark, the owner, and I discussed the need to replicate the original patterns. With the old interior, an authenticity manual and some research, we had all the tools to make this happen. The interior turned out beautifully. I would venture to say it is probably better than when produced.

As with any restoration project, the process is painstaking, always longer than expected and over budget, but the finished product seemed to overpower the memory of the restoration pitfalls.

The first showing

When I received the May 2008 issue of "The Self Starter," I realized the Cadillac & LaSalle Club Grand Nationals were going to be held in nearby Cherry Hill, N.J., from Aug. 1-4. The goal now was to complete the Cadillac in time for the show. I had registered the car with hopes of completing the restoration prior to the big weekend in Cherry Hill, and it was completed one week before Aug. 1; this did not leave a lot of time for preparation.

I decided to trailer the car to the show. This was the first official car show experience with a car for my son and I. It was also the first showing of the car. We had a great time and had the benefit of interaction with many car enthusiasts from around the country.

We entered the Cadillac in the primary class, P9. I received a call several weeks after the show to inform me that we placed first in the P9 class and the car would be receiving a senior badge and trophy. Needless to say, this was the rainbow after the storm. I hope my son Gianni keeps and maintains this work of art and preserves the glory of the 1936 Cadillac Series 60 coupe. After all, it is the "Standard of the World."

THE 3-MILLIONTH V-8 FORD VISITED BIG 'D'

A crowd surrounds the 3 millionth Ford V-8 in 1936 as it stopped at the Texas Pavilion in Dallas during the state's centennial. The crowd is dressed in white to combat the hot Texas summer. The 1936 Deluxe Fordor had chromed wheels highlighted by whitewall tires that matched the well-dressed crowd.

Well-known automotive artist Bob Eng has a fine collection of photographs from his father-in-law's collection. The photos depict a very important 1936 Ford: the 3 millionth V-8 produced.

Reaching 3 million V-8s by 1936 was a truly astonishing feat considering the V-8 had only been introduced in 1932, just four years earlier and in the very depths of the Great Depression. In those four years, the economy had not been kind to Americans. The country remained in the throes of the depression and independent car makers were melting away like ice cubes in the Texas heat. Add in the fact that four-cylinders were also built by Ford until August

Presumably before the 3 millionth V-8's journey, it posed at the factory in Dearborn with Henry (left) and Edsel (far right). In the background are Ford Tudor and Fordor bodies that appear ready to complete the "body drop."

A bannered 1936 Ford phaeton (background at right) was prepared to greet the 3 millionth Ford V-8 upon its arrival at the Texas Pavilion. The 3 millionth's entourage at the Texas Pavilion included several new V-12 Lincoln-Zephyr models, as well as other new 1936 Fords. A large Texaco sign hangs in the background.

When the 3 millionth V-8 Ford was built in 1936, it toured the country, gathering its own series of license plates. The historic Ford is pictured here while in Texas.

1934, and the V-8's amazing production numbers seem even more unlikely.

These photos depict the 3 millionth V-8 Ford, a 1936 Deluxe Fordor, during its stop at the Texas Pavilion, held in Dallas in honor of the Lone Star State's centennial. In addition to the landmark car, there are some other very important Fords in these photos, namely Henry and Edsel. Eng's father-in-law had these photos because he also had an important part in the Ford exposition: he was a chef for Ford Motor Co. while the company toured with its automobiles that year.

We're glad he came away with more than a sense of pride for his work at the exposition. He came away with these photos to share as well.

By Brian Earnest

ONCE BITTEN

1936 Packard 120 is love at first sight for new hobbyist

Dennis Frank's first hobby car is a beauty: a nicely restored 1936 Packard 120. The 120s remain highly popular among collectors and were Packard's first medium-priced car when they were introduced in 1935.

Dennis Frank had never been an "official" car hobbyist before, but he had secretly admired many old cars from afar — particularly big Classic Era cars that he figured would always be out of his league.

But when the Prophetstown, Ill., resident finally decided to jump into the collector car game, he went "all in" — opting for a lovely restored 1936 Packard 120 touring coupe that has quickly become the neatest toy he's ever owned.

"I always thought, 'Boy, if I could ever find one, I'd love to own one,'" said Frank, who became a Packard owner for the first time earlier this year. "I have always been amazed at the way people have kept and

The unique "Queen's Truck" trunk arrangement featured
a spare tire compartment below the regular trunk.

preserved these cars. I just love this car.

"I was looking for a '49, but I couldn't find one, and then I came across this '36. The guy who owned it lived in Elkhorn, Wis., and from the pictures it almost looked too good to be true. So I went up and visited him, and when I saw it I couldn't believe it then, either."

According to the story Frank got, the car had been pulled from a garage in the Chicago area back in the 1980s and eventually received a substantial restoration. The work included new Pale Butter Yellow paint with Hunter Green pinstriping, a new vinyl roof, new window glass and rubber, new interior, and new rings and bearings in the Packard's original straight-eight engine.

"The odometer has only got about 31,000 miles on it, but there is no way to know if that's original or not," Frank said. "The owners had the motor all rebuilt. The running boards were gone and a lot of other pieces were gone. The only thing that hasn't been restored is the dash. That's all original. The steering wheel was kind of cracked and messed up, so that's been epoxied up.

"He had spent the past 10 or 12 years working on it. He had everything re-chromed and put back on the car. I still need about three pieces to make it all complete. I need to find some bumper guards for the back, and the driver's door handle — somebody made

one and it looks almost exactly right, but we still need to find a door handle for it."

Frank's car has one other peculiarity — it was given the unique "Queen's Truck" trunk arrangement. "They call it that because the trunk is on the top and on the bottom there is another door. The spare tire is under there. On normal Packards you open the trunk and the spare tire is right there, but this has another door.

"The people that used to own the car took it go Warren, Ohio, for Packard's 100th anniversary and the people there told them that there were only about five of these in the United States. It's pretty unique."

When it introduced the medium-priced 120 series in 1935, however, Packard wasn't targeting any queens or other royalty. It was

the first time the high-end automaker took a stab at a machine that the average American could actually consider owning. The bottom-tier 120s were definitely not strippers or economy cars, but for less than $1,100, buyers could take home one of seven different '35 Packards, and only the five-passenger convertible sedan and five-passenger touring sedan exceeded $1,100 for 1936. That meant you could actually buy two of the "junior" Packards for the price of a single 1400 model — the next tier up in the Packard hierarchy.

This was big news for Packard and an important step in the company's evolution. During the Great Depression, the demand for luxury cars slowed to a trickle, and Packard needed a new, more-affordable of-

The Packard 120s came with a 120-hp straight-eight under the hood.

fering or risk going out of business. The 120 filled the bill. It was warmly received at the time — more than 55,000 120s were built for 1936 after 25,000 were sold during the car's rookie year — and the 120 remains of a favorite of collectors and car buffs today.

Many Packard fans — back in the 1930s and today — actually preferred the 120 series to the "senior" cars. They were lighter, steered and stopped better, were easier to own and maintain and, in the opinion of some drivers, rode better than the hulking Eights, Super Eights and Twelves.

Frank's touring coupe carried a sticker price of about $1,040 when it rolled off the lot, and for that the lucky buyer got a hand-

some 3,475-lb. car that carried the standard 384-cid, 120-hp L-head straight-eight, a selective synchromesh transmission, 7 x 16-inch tires riding on a 120-inch wheelbase and hydraulic brakes.

"It's pretty basic," Frank said. "There's no clock in it, just a regular speedometer, amp-meter and temperature [gauge], and a glove box. That's it. Oh, and it's got a heater.

"The biggest thing for me is just the way it looks. I love the body style, the head-lights… just everything about it".

Frank said he didn't have a show pony in mind when he decided to get a collector car. He wanted a car that would be road-worthy and fun to drive whenever the spirit moved

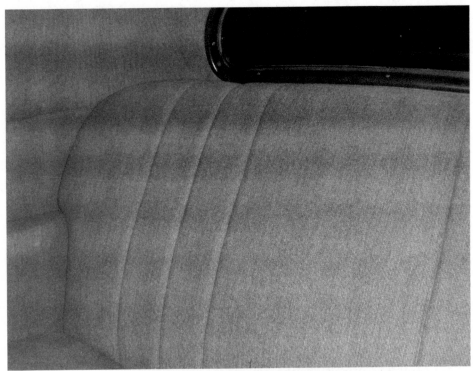

The cloth interior has been re-done, including the lovely backseat.

him. After he worked out some initial bugs, the Packard hasn't disappointed.

"It wasn't running too good when I first got it because it had apparently been sitting for awhile. It would run nice and smooth at first, but at about 30 [mph] it would hesitate," he said. "But now I've got it running a lot better, and it runs great down the highway. You just go!

"Of course, with those narrow tires, you gotta be careful because any groove in the road, those wheels can grab and just follow."

Frank says the "dings" and other imper-fections that remain on the car don't bother him a bit. In fact, it's the car's little warts that make it the ideal Sunday driver. "Oh, it's got a few things that need to be touched up, but that's what I like about it. It's not in such excellent shape that you can't drive it," he said. "I don't want a car that you put on a trailer and haul around because it's so pristine that you don't want to wreck it.

"For a car that is 74 years old, it's in pret-ty darn good shape. It's still here, somebody took the time to fix it up and keep it that way, and that's what I plan to do, too."

DASHING DARRIN

Stunning one-off 1937 cabriolet is part Ford, part Darrin

1937 FORD DARRIN
MODEL 78 CABRIOLET

COURTESY OF J.B. SAUNDERS,
OKLAHOMA

Although the single 1937 Ford Darrin followed the 1936 Jensen Fords, the cars have a common ancestor. Today, this one-of-a-kind 1937 Ford victoria is owned by J.B. Saunders, who had it restored to concours condition.

Howard "Dutch" Darrin remains known for the custom coachwork on such fine motor cars as Minerva, Rolls-Royce and Isotta Fraschini while he was teamed in the Paris-based firms Hibbard & Darrin and Fernandez & Darrin. But, it's the Packard Darrin victoria that has become his signature model. After the Darrin-bodied Packards, the designer further contributed to the styling of prewar Packard Clippers and postwar Kaisers and Frazers, particularly the Kaiser Darrin sports car. Often forgotten among these giants is the lone Ford victoria that predated the famed Darrin Packards built from 1938-'42.

In the mid 1930s, the American-born Darrin moved from Paris to Southern California and established Darrin of Paris in Hollywood. The first Darrin produced in the United States was not based on a

THE FIRST DARRIN AUTOMOBILE PRODUCED IN THIS COUNTRY WAS THIS 1937 FORD
OWNED BY J.B. SAUNDERS

The Ford Darrin as it appeared in the early days (above) and today (right).

high-priced Duesenberg or Minerva, but on a "lowly" Ford Model 78 Cabriolet. This one-off Ford Darrin makes an interesting, if sometimes confusing, story. Fortunately, Robert Knee, a historian at the Automotive Driving Museum in El Segundo, Calif., has done extensive research to tell the complete story of the Ford Darrin. This was done as part of the museum's "Darrin Style" exhibit that will run until Aug. 1, 2010.

Movie mogul Darryl Zanuck, whom Darrin met while in Paris, was instrumental in getting Darrin to move to Hollywood. Zanuck would also become a key link to Darrin of Paris' main customers — Hollywood celebrities. Darrin's automotive reputation likely helped him become friends

The Darrin Ford in front of the Al Nerney Ford dealership that probably supplied its chassis, as the dealership had previously done for the Jensen Ford.

with L.A. restaraunteur Percy Morgan, who was also in the business of purchasing Ford chassis from Al Nerney Ford in Los Angeles and then shipping them to Jensen Motors in England. There, the Fords were built into Jensen Ford victorias before they were sent back to Morgan.

Darrin had Morgan build a similar type of car, but with Darrin styling, on a Ford chassis. It looked a bit like the Jensen Ford, which is likely the source of the myth that more than one Ford Darrin was built. Incidentally, while Clark Gable did order a silver Jensen Ford, he never took delivery. However, Gable did pose with one for photos to help Morgan sell the Jensen Fords.

According to Knee, the 1937 Ford Darrin was probably built at Newels body shop

in Los Angeles. (The Darrin of Paris location 8860 Sunset Blvd did not exist yet.) This Ford also sported the famous "Darrin dip" in the rear portion of the doors, another trademark of "Dutch" Darrin.

Percy Morgan was the first owner of this car, the only Darrin-bodied Ford known to have been built. Shortly after the unique 1937 Ford was constructed, Morgan and Darrin decided that Packard would be a better platform upon which to build these victorias, since they were aimed at a Hollywood clientele. Additionally, the Packard chassis was only slightly more than the Ford chassis.

In the late 1930s, Irving Fogle acquired this Ford Darrin from Morgan. R.J. "Bob" White, a close friend of Fogle, loved the

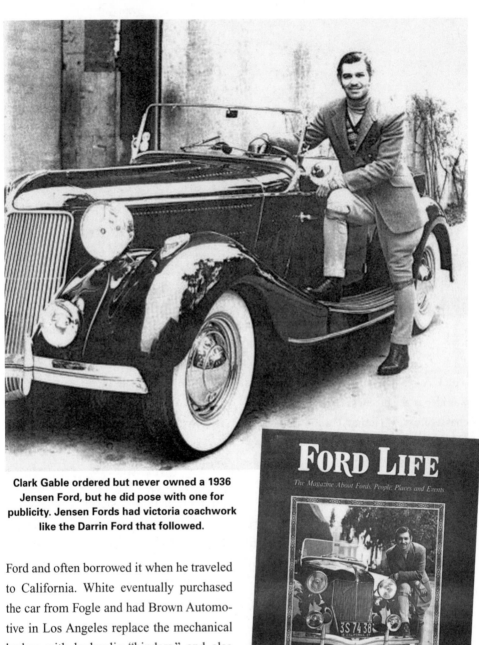

Clark Gable ordered but never owned a 1936 Jensen Ford, but he did pose with one for publicity. Jensen Fords had victoria coachwork like the Darrin Ford that followed.

Ford and often borrowed it when he traveled to California. White eventually purchased the car from Fogle and had Brown Automotive in Los Angeles replace the mechanical brakes with hydraulic "binders," and also had Stromberg 97's installed on a dual-carburetor manifold. The engine was rebuilt and the car was also repainted and re-upholstered. Then, it disappeared.

The Ford Darrin had the characteristic "Darrin Dip" door styling. The wood dashboard was custom made.

In 1968, J.B. Saunders, the current owner of the Ford Darrin, discovered the car when he heard of a Cord convertible in Oklahoma City. The Cord turned out to be a sedan in poor condition. Peering through the slats of an old storage shed while searching out the Cord, Saunders saw what appeared to be a modified 1937 Ford convertible under a pile of boxes. A hubcap had the "Darrin" script on it and he investigated it further. He found the car belonged to Orta May White, Bob White's widow. In 1969, Saun-

Packards were known more for their Darrin bodies than Ford, but the first Darrin came from Ford. Above is a 1942 Packard Darrin.

ders bought the car from White's widow and was able to contact previous owner Irving Fogel, who supplied details regarding the car's history.

This fabulous "barn find" was complete down to the hubcaps, and with very little rust. However, the wood, particularly in the instrument panel and doors, was in poor condition. Saunders partially restored it over the years, then started a more comprehensive restoration in 2003 that was completed in 2006. Since then, the Ford Darrin has appeared in many car concours events, including the 2003 Pebble Beach Concours d'Elegance and the 2006 Amelia Island Concours d'Elegance in 2006.

Knee has also busted other myths about the Darrin Ford. It was not powered by a Mercury Flathead V-8, but retained the stock Ford Flathead V-8. Also, it was built on a 1937 chassis, as noted by serial numbers on the frame and engine, not a 1936 model. However, it does have 1936 rear fenders, which probably added to the confusion of the car's build date.

Some of the styling cues from the Ford Darrin were carried over to the Packard Darrin victoria, the first of which was built for Dick Powell. Other Darrin Victorias were built for Clark Gable, Tyrone Power,

The Darrin Ford was built on a 1937 Frd chassis, but it does have 1936 rear fenders.

Errol Flynn, Al Jolson, Rosalind Russell, Preston Foster, Ann Sheridan, Constance Bennett, Gene Krupa and several other top Hollywood celebrities.

For the victoria, the top was cut off Packard One Ten business coupes bought from a Texas dealer for $1,100. By retaining many parts from the donor coupes and some very innovative cost-cutting manufacturing techniques, Packard Darrins could be delivered to Packard dealers for $3,200-$3,300. The dealers then added their mark-up.

In 1939, Dutch Darrin left Southern California and moved to Connersville, Ind., to better supply Packard with his custom body models. However, his craftsmen and designers preferred California to eastern weather and stayed here. They founded Coachcraft Ltd., led by Rudy Stoessel, Darrin of Paris' former foreman. Coachcraft, which is still in business in Fillmore, Calif., being run by Rudy's son Bill, built about a dozen customs.

By Gerald Perschbacher

1937 WAS A GREAT YEAR TO OWN A PACKARD

Banner year marked the high point for the company's prestige and success

A bevy of beauties flank and fondle a new 1937 Packard. Seldom did the Packard Motor Car Company use swimsuit models to stage new cars, but this rare shot seems to capture the fondness the general public held for Packard in its best year.

1937 was a very good year for the Packard Motor Car Company. In fact, it was its best.

Sales were hot. Styling was grand. Appointments were superb. Packard was one of the most desired names in the public mind. The only other automotive name that grabbed the attention of the citizenry with any similar degree was Ford, a name relegated to the lower-price field of cars. Not so with Packard. If there was any name that represented royalty among cars, it was Packard.

More than a thousand distinguished families in America claimed Packard ownership for 22 years or more. Such impetus churned the public to covet a Packard. Didn't matter what stratum of society a person inhabited. This was the car to adore and respect with legendary honors.

That especially was the case in 1937 when the Detroit-based company introduced its Six. With its launch, the Packard name was accessible to anyone who could afford to buy a new car. Priced below $1,000, the Packard Six carried all the design traits that the public demanded in a conservative, stately car. It was just smaller, less powerful and not as fancy. But it looked every bit a Packard. No one denied its lineage. If a buyer was contemplating a Ford, Chevy or Plymouth, less than a couple hundred dollars separated that choice from all the good graces a Packard Six delivered to the buyer's curb.

Every new Packard for 1937 carried a frontal appearance that resembled timeless classic Roman or Greek architecture. Reminiscent of ancient columns, long grille louvers automatically opened or closed to regulate radiator temperature on senior cars that boasted straight-eight power and simplicity or V-12 elegance.

If a buyer craved more than the Six, the next step was a One-Twenty powered by the company's smallest straight eight. The car offered huge benefits in the slightly more than $1,000 range. This was the car for rising executives and women of increased influence. It commanded respect on the road. Dealers made owners feel special as an investment on the future. With the sale of every One-Twenty, Packard officials hoped the buyer would be successful enough to soon trade it on the next step in the Packard stairwell: the Super Eight.

Priced at $2,300 on up, the Super Eight was a larger, roomier car, manly in most respects, but sufficiently outfitted to attract the longing eyes of women who preferred quality in fit, finish and tactile appointments. "Open the hood to sell the man; open the door to sell the woman," ran a saying among Packard salesmen. The Super Eight delivered as much power and speed as most drivers of the day wanted and most roads of the time allowed.

Economy was not a major concern if you could afford a senior Packard, but it lingered as a small issue amid the up-and-down years of the economically challenged 1930s. A Super Eight, properly tuned and maintained, then driven conscientiously, could be expected to deliver 12 to 18 miles per gallon under good driving conditions.

Perched atop the entire Packard stairway was the magnificent Twelve priced as low as $3,400. Gas mileage concerns evap-

The 1937 lineup for Packard: from left, the Six, the Super-Eight, the Twelve and the One-Twenty. There were several body styles in each line, with custom-bodied cars available even on junior models. For some reason, the company chose three four-door sedans and one two-door for this publicity shot.

orated to the winds as these nearly three-ton cars often gulped fuel as they delivered 8-12 miles per gallon. So be it. Even as the Great Depression still gripped America, there were some families that gained wealth. Why shouldn't they have enjoyed their success?

Some did so at the risk of rock assaults if their Twelves motored through the wrong parts of poverty-stricken towns. Even this did not keep Packard from registering its best production year for V-12 models: 1,300 were made.

The Twelves were palaces on wheels. Extremely high-quality wool upholstery materials were specially selected. Leather appointments, such as padded tops on Formal Sedans or leather front compartments on limousines, commanded the best in hides and workmanship. Twelves were

tested by Packard throughout the 250-mile break-in period, then made ready for final inspection before being delivered to new owners.

In 1937, "Ask the Man Who Owns One" became a motto for 2.74 percent of the buying public. Calendar year sales surpassed 109,000 units. Never before had Packard reached that level. Never would it reach it again.

As expected, the Twelve claimed the most modest slice of the pie at around 1.2 percent, with Super Eight taking a portion at 4.8 percent. One-Twenty production had a generous 41 percent. The darling newcomer Six expectedly hoarded the majority of the pie with 53 percent.

Custom-ordered cars were an option. Buyers selected from various books and photographs supplied by Packard or

The 1937 Packard Super Eight Victoria

by custom-body design houses. Among the most popular were Dietrich and Derham, although any custom builder had the chance to display their talents on a Packard chassis. Most customs were designed for Twelves and Supers. A handful was made on the One-Twenty chassis. Rumor has it that even an occasional Six may have been contemplated, although Packard officials probably did not encourage such acts.

If power and dimensions were determining factors for buyers, then a glance in the statistics column provided cheat-sheet facts: the Six offered a wheelbase of 115 inches cradling an engine of 237 cubic inches delivering 100 horsepower. The One-Twenty offered a 120-inch wheelbase hosting a 282-cubic-inch engine pounding out 120 horsepower. The Super Eight's wheelbase began at 127 inches and framed the 320-cubic-inch engine producing 130 to 135 horsepower. The Twelve's wheelbases ran from 132 to 144 inches and bolstered the 473-cubic-inch engine which gave a walloping 175 horsepower.

In 1937, the master of a massive estate could call for Chauffeur Jeeves to pull the Packard Twelve Formal Sedan out of the converted carriage house and station it in the front door's drive to await departure. Junior could brag about his Super Eight convertible coupe with rumble seat that was ready for the daily drive to varsity events. Sis had her One-Twenty Club Sedan to take her through the entrance drive of the exclusive finishing school. Even the gardener could drive to and fro in his own Packard Six sedan feeling pretty special, meeting his master on the road while flashing all the good characteristic of Packard success.

In 1937, all good things, automotively speaking, could be yours in a Packard!

REBORN WILLYS

'37 sedan goes from the barn to the Blue Ribbon corral

Earl Pamperin spent eight years bringing his 1937 Willys back to life. Original Willys from the era are scarce due to their relatively low production numbers and the Willys' popularity among racers and street-rodders.

Earl Pamperin admits he probably didn't fully understand what he was getting himself into when he decided to bring his rare 1937 Willys sedan back to life almost 25 years ago.

That's probably a good thing, because he might have been scared off if he had fully grasped how challenging it would be.

"It was the first car I've done. It took me eight years. I guess when I look back on it, you'd rather have started with a complete Pierce or something" laughed Pamperin, a resident of Juneau, Wis.

The car was actually a bit of a barn find, at least for Pamperin, back in 1981. That was the year he got married and saw the car for the first time. "[My wife's] late husband had bought it from the estate of a dentist,"

Pamperin said. "They had bought it, used it in their wedding and kind of done an Earl Scheib kind of paint job on it, just so they could drive it. Then he died — he was killed in a car accident — and the car sat in a barn until I met her.

"She took me over to see it one day, and I thought, 'Geez, that would be a good car to have at home." It sat there for a good two years after we got married … but we eventually dragged it home and I started going to car shows in about '86, looking around and seeing what guys were doing."

What most guys were doing at the time, and had been doing for years, was turning the small and economic Willys of that time period into street machines and hot rods. Custom Willys from the era are not hard to

find, but all-steel and original '37s are another story.

Pamperin knew immediately that the couple's '37 was not destined for an engine transplant, tubbed rear end or flame paint job. "I wasn't really happy with all the cars guys were cutting up to make into hot rods," he said. "I thought there was too much car there to start cutting on it."

That Willys cars from the late-1930s are rare and desirable today is an unlikely story in itself. Even with a complete redesign that year, the 1937 Willys car lineup was far from the most outwardly attractive menu on the new car scene. Still, there has been something appealing and enduring about the Willys' more rounded lines and sloping roof lines. Street rodders have found the

Above, the upholstery on the venerable Willys is all new after "we found, like, seven nests of mice in there from the barn," said Pamperin. Below, the simple two-pod dash features a round speedometer (right) and a second gauge that displays fuel level, oil temperature and amps.

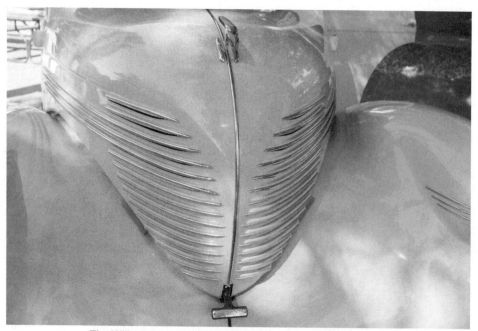

The Willys' curved hood was decorated by horizontal spears bisected by a chrome strip running down the center.

cars' short wheelbase and light weight help them go fast, and in recent years, restorers have found the cars worthy candidates for extensive back-to-original resurrections.

Willys had introduced its small, simple, four-cylinder Model 77 in 1933. Production numbers during those Depression years were tiny, and less than 45,000 Model 77s were built over the span of four years before the lineup got a new look in 1937.

That year, the Willys was given a blunt grille with a rounded nose, as well as headlamps in pods mounted atop the fenders. The new car was christened the Model 37, and more than 51,400 were built for the model year, although production figures

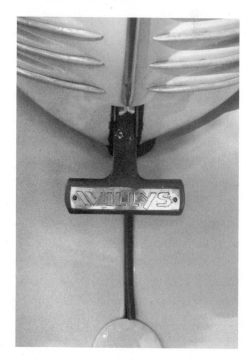

Under the hood of the '37 Willys was the holdover 134-cid, 48-hp four-cylinder.

seem to vary depending on your source.

The car's holdover 134-cubic-inch L-head four produced a modest 48 hp and shifted through a three-speed manual transmission. The cars eventually became somewhat unlikely favorites of weekend racers, who installed overhead-valve V-8s in the original Willys chassis, while keeping the sleek, lightweight body. Eventually, the "gasser" Willys cars would become beloved icons of the street and strip, particularly the 1941 coupes.

The Model 37 ran on 100-inch wheelbases with hydraulic drum brakes at all four corners and semi-elliptical leaf springs softening the harsh ride of the front and rear solid axles.

Aside from its general shape and profile, perhaps the 1937-'38 Willys' most identifying feature was the assemblage of narrow, chrome spears that ran horizontally backwards from the nose. The spears were bisected up the center of the hood by another lengthy chrome piece that reached from the windshield to the bottom edge of the curved bow.

"When we got the car, there was a bag full of those chrome strips in the trunk," Pamperin said. "But they weren't on the car. The guy who had done some bodywork on this car in the past had even filled up the holes for the strips. When I stripped the car all down, these holes were there.

"What happened at the time was that,

of course, Willys was going in and out of receivership and they were having financial problems, so the factory was sending the cars out and promising the dealers they would send these chrome strips along. And, of course, that didn't always happen."

The arrangement did provide Pamperin with enough trim pieces to reconstruct most of his Willys grille work, although he did have to order some more stainless and get some of the pieces made. The trim bits weren't the only things Pamperin had to tackle. The car needed new floors throughout, a new interior and plenty of elbow grease on the body.

"We tore it all down and I got a guy to start the bodywork, but he lost interest," Pamperin said. "He had worked on the actual body, and then sort of threw it back to me. Well, after watching him I figured I could do all the stuff he was doing. I took all the fenders and doors and I did all the bodywork on all that. Then I met a body guy and he kind of showed me how to get it to look nice …

"I couldn't salvage anything in the interior. There had been mice in it. I think we found, like, seven nests of mice in there from the barn. So I took it to a guy in Fort Atkinson [Wis.] and he did all the new upholstery."

And, of course, there was the requisite amount of salvage yard visits, Internet browsing and swap meet networking involved in any challenging restoration. Genuine Willys parts are not easy to come by, but Pamperin stuck with it until he found almost everything he needed.

"It was just a progression of things and finding stuff. I found a guy in Pennsylvania that had these 'new old stock' hubcaps. And I found a guy in San Francisco that had these beauty rings, and another guy had a steering wheel. A guy in Los Angeles, he calls himself Willys Replacement Parts — you can get a lot of stuff from him.

"I sent the bumpers out to have them re-plated. I had the frame sandblasted and painted and we started from there, building up the springs … My body man friend painted it, and I had the engine rebuilt, but I pretty much did everything else myself."

The engine in his '37 is not factory issued, according to Pamperin. "We don't think it's the original motor, because it's got the word 'Jeep' on it, and they didn't use the word 'Jeep' until World War II," he said. "So we think somebody had trouble and replaced the motor at some time. I'm thinking it would have been an early '40s. It might have happened in the late '40s and they put a motor from the early '40s in it.

In a nod to non-originality and better performance, Pamperin also put a non-stock carburetor and intake on the Willys, mainly so the car could keep up better on the highway.

"It ran OK up until about 40-45 [mph], but I wasn't happy with it beyond that," he said. "So I ran into a guy who said 'I've got

a carburetor that will fix that for you,' so I got a Carter carburetor for it. The original manifold was actually cracked and I went to a junkyard and robbed an intake and exhaust from an old Jeep Wagoneer, I think it was, from the early '50s. The Carter carburetor matched that intake, so it's got a bigger hole in the intake. Now it does 55 easy.

"But it's got to be a relatively smooth road," he added with a chuckle. "With those solid axles, you hit a bump at 50, it's rough."

Pamperin discovered during his work on the body that the car wore tan paint when it left the factory, so that's what it wears today. The tan interior adds to the sedan's low-key appearance, which is OK with Pamperin.

He doesn't mind if the car doesn't necessarily get all the attention such a rare survivor probably deserves.

"People don't know what it is, or they walk by it because they don't really notice it too much," he said. "Or they ask me about the color and say, 'Why did you paint it primer color?'"

Pamperin certainly never set out to make a museum quality showpiece out of his Willys, but the car did spend three years in the Wisconsin Automotive Museum in Hartford, Wis., after he completed its restoration. "Yeah, we were doing an addition on our house and putting all the kitchen stuff in the garage," he said. "So that worked out pretty good!"

STUDEBAKER STOOD FIRM IN '37-38

Donald Douglas, of McDonald-Douglas Aircraft fame, was a big fan of the 1937 Studebakers and drove this four-door sedan dressed up with white sidewall tires and bright metal wheel trim rings.

Not many 1937 automakers would perch a 10,000-lb. cement silo on the roof of a sedan, but Studebaker had a knack for doing stunts that other companies shied away from. Although the silo pushed the running boards close to the ground, the doors of the car retained their ability to easily open and close. "The safety steel-reinforced-by-steel Studebaker body with the world's largest one-piece steel top stood up unharmed," said an advertisement featuring this unusual promotion.

Airplane designer Donald Douglas was a Studebaker fan and the owner of a similar sedan. "I can't see how anyone would want any more in a car," he said. A one-

The 1937 Studebaker was promoted as an "exciting" car that cost only a little more than the lowest-priced cars and gave comparable gas and oil economy.

piece cowl-hinged hood and a slanting and rounded radiator shell with horizontal grille bars were styling traits of all 17 models that Studebaker offered in 1937.

The cars included seven Dictator Six models priced from $765 to $900 and powered by a 217.8-cid in-line six that made 90 horsepower. The body types included a Business Coupe, three- and five-passenger Custom Coupes, Custom and Cruising Sedans in standard St. Regis trim and Custom and Cruising Sedans in top-of-the-line trim. ("Cruising Sedan" was Studebaker's name for a sedan with a built-in trunk.) All of the sixes shared a 116-inch wheelbase. All were available in a 6-A Series that added

independent Planar Front Wheel suspension for $20.

This suspension was included with the larger President Eight models that came in the same body styles, less the Business Coupe, at prices from $1,085 to $1,185. Four body types including the Custom Coupes, Custom Sedan and Cruising Sedan were also available with upscale State trim for $30 additional. The 250.4-cid Studebaker straight eight produced 115 hp at 3,600 rpm. With a 125-inch wheelbase, the Presidents were larger cars and needed the extra power to move their added bulk.

Studebaker was the first car to offer motorists the double safety of the automatic hill

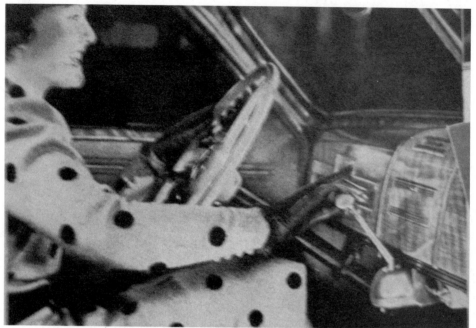

Studebaker's new-for-1938 Miracle Shift was actuated by vacuum but worked like a floor shift without blocking the center of the front compartment. This feature was optional on all 1938 models.

holder and feather-touch hydraulic brakes. Standard equipment also included a Fram oil filter, automatic overdrive and doors that closed tightly and silently on revolutionary new rattle-proof rotary latches. Studebaker used a 12-coatdeep paint finish on its cars and offered a C.I.T. budget plan for buyers who wanted to purchase cars via low-cost time payments.

Time-payment plans were important in the years that saw the Great Depression winding down and the economy perking up again. The same was true of fuel mileage. Studebaker Dictator Sixes were noted for their efficiency and achieved 27.46 mpg

under American Automobile Association supervision at the Bonneville Salt Flats.

Other "Spotlight" features of the 1937 Studebaker included a new steering gear that halved the turning effort required for parking and rounded "Air Curved" body styling. A gifted designer named Helen Dryden was charged with fashioning Studebaker's "lavishly roomy" interiors. Their were chair-high seats for driver and passenger comfort and an enormously spacious luggage compartment.

Exclusive looks and low-priced luxury were Studebaker's headliners for 1938. On all models, louvers were eliminated from

This 1938 Studebaker Commander coupe might have been a hit at the beach, but it only had room for three.

the hood side panels and the hill-holder feature was standard. Studebaker's new Miracle Shift vacuum-operated gearshift was an option for all models. Though it operated in the same manner as a floor shift, it left the front floor clear and provided added roominess for the driver and passenger riding "shotgun."

Independent planar wheel front suspension was now a regular Studebaker feature, along with outstanding shock absorbers, symmetrical direct-action steering, twin windshield wipers, twin tail lamps, twin sun visors, rattle-proof rotary door latches, safety glass all around, a new "horizontal" transmission and an under-slung hypoid gear rear axle.

The Dictator name for the six-cylinder cars was replaced by Commander. The low-priced Commander six offered a Business Coupe, Club Coupe, Club Sedan, Cruising Sedan and Convertible Sedan for $875 to $1,315. All four body styles were also offered in State Commander trim for higher prices up to $1,365. A larger 226-cid six was installed, but output remained at 90 horsepower. The wheelbase grew just a half inch.

The President Eight lineup included a three-passenger Coupe for $1,120, a six-passenger Club Sedan for $1,185 and a Cruising Sedan for $1,195. All three, plus a Convertible Sedan, came in richer State President format for $10 additional ($1,555 for the Convertible Sedan). The eight-cylinder wheelbase shrunk to 122 inches and the 250-cid straight-eight carried a lowered 110-hp rating.

By Brian Earnest

BACK FROM THE BARN

1938 Chevrolet Master Business Coupe was a long time coming

Richard Thomas' 1938 Chevy coupe is in a lot better shape today than it was about five years ago when he bought it (above). Thomas had known about the car for many years, and finally got the chance to own it after the car had been slumbering for many years in a farm shed.

Richard Thomas waited a long time to land his "Sweetie." More than four decades in fact. And when opportunity finally knocked, even at the least-expected time and most unlikely place, he didn't hesitate.

Thomas had known about the 1938 Chevrolet Master Business Coupe since he and the car's owner were childhood friends back in the 1960s. Even though he didn't own other collector cars and wasn't active in the car hobby, Thomas had always told his friend, Mike Webb, that he'd like to buy his car someday. He was always rebuffed, until his luck finally began to change in late 2003. The two men bumped into each other at a garage sale after not seeing each other for many years, and Thomas again gave Webb his sales pitch. A year later, Thomas called him on the phone, still pining for the car. Then, finally, in December of 2004, the pair saw each other at another garage sale, and this time, Webb's tune had changed.

"I think he had hoped and hoped that he'd get around to restoring it, but his health was getting bad," said Thomas, a resident of Arkansas City, Kan. "Life isn't always fair, and it wasn't fair to him. He was having some hard times.

"But I was very surprised that he agreed to sell it to me. I could hardly believe it."

It would seem no great surprise that Webb would have trouble parting with the car he had owned for so many years. He had gotten the car from the original owner, Elijah Ham, who had purchased the car new from a fledgling dealership in Arkansas City. Ham, a friend of the Webb family, apparently drove the car very little, and during his retirement years decided to give the car to Mike Webb, who was just 14 at the time. Thomas says the other boys didn't know Webb even had such a car, but he remembers the day everyone found out!

The old Chevy had been left in a barn and was covered in dirt. The interior was shot, but the body was solid enough to save.

"The first first time I saw it just a bunch of us guys 17, 18 years old, right in that area, we were just hanging out and doing what teenagers did in the '60s," he said. "I didn't even know he had it. I about died when I saw it. It was just a cool old car. Of course, we didn't really know much about it, I just thought it was cool.

"[He] let us all drool, then took it back to the house. He'd get it out on occasion. But he eventually had a little problem with the brakes — the positive battery cable rubbed a hole in the brake line. And one day he popped the brakes and ran into the back of a flatbed truck and put a nice crease in the grille. After that he rolled her into the barn and there she sat ...

"It just stayed in the barn and as time went on, we both went our own ways and didn't much of each other. ... Every once in a while we'd pass ways and I'd kind of half-heartedly say, "Hey, want to sell me that car yet?"

By the time Thomas got his chance to own the car, which he calls his "Sweetie," it had sat for more than 20 years. The gas had turned "to varnish" and the neglected Chevy was covered with a thick layer of dust. It had also become home to generations of unidentified varmints and various other creatures. It was a long way from the impressive, shiny coupe that Thomas remembered from his teenage years.

"I was kind of hoping it would be in that kind of shape where it had been setting for a while, but wasn't let go as much as it had been," he said. "I was hoping to change the oil, put a fresh battery in it and go for a ride. But that was not the case."

Chevrolet's "diamond crown" styling changes were introduced for the 1937 mod-

els and carried over into 1938. The changes included safety glass in all the windows and fenders that were straight on the sides. The '38s had a new grille that alternated narrow and wide horizontal bars with a center molding down the middle. There were a few other styling tweaks for the '38s, but the body shells and running boards were the same on the '37s and '38s.

The hoods had ventilators with three chrome horizontal moldings. The headlamps were bullet-shaped and mounted close to the grille. Master series cars — there was also a higher-end Master Deluxe series — hand single tail lamps.

Under the hood was the familiar Chevy inline six, displacing 216.5 cubic inches and producing a modest 85 hp. A three-speed manual transmission with the stick on the floor was standard on all the bowtie '38s.

There were a total of 12 different Chevrolets available in 1938 — six each in both the Master and Master Deluxe lineups. The two-door town sedans were the most popular by far with 95,050 built, but coupes were also good sellers. A total of 39,793 coupes like Thomas' rolled off Chevy assembly lines carrying base prices of $648, which was the lowest MSRP on the Chevy menu.

Thomas began to bring his Sweetie back to life. He started by fixing the starter and fuel pump, but then made a costly mistake when he started the car without cleaning out the old gas tank.

"I finally did get it started. It ran — it

was a little rough — but it did run," he recalls. "Well, after I got done bouncing off the walls with excitement, I took a couple of pictures of it running, then I shut it off and went inside. The next day I went out to start it again, it just went [insert loud engine noise sounds]! Come to find out the fresh gas I had put in it had melted enough varnish and the varnish

had gotten up into the engine and stuck the valves shut. Overnight it had crystallized right in the engine. I had to buy a whole new set of push rods and whole set of lifters … Now I preach that hard, hard: If you ever buy a car that hasn't been started in a long time, before you start it, pull the tank on it and clean it all out. You'll save yourself a lot of problems."

The next big step in what Thomas termed "a rolling restoration" was to replace much of the interior "so it didn't smell like a bathroom," he said. "I drove it that way for a while and actually took it to some shows. It was all pretty much original, except for the interior.

"Most of paint had popped off it. It had a lot of bare spots and lot of surface rust. I still had fun driving it and darn sure didn't have to worry about polishing it before went a show."

Thomas kept massaging the old '38 at a little at a time, fixing and replacing a few

body panels, then priming the back half of the car and re-chroming the rear bumper. "From the side it looked kind of funny," he said. "The back half looked good and front half was all original."

Thomas eventually primed the front half of the car, too, and got the rest of the chrome done. "It had aftermarket fender shirts on it so it looked like a low-rider. It really looked cool!" he said.

The finishing touch finally came last winter when the car got a shiny new suit of black paint. "I decided to bite the bullet," Thomas said. The car is now arguably better than new, with options like fender skirts, heater, defroster, clock and ashtray that were not in the car when it was ordered new.

After waiting all these years, Thomas has no problems putting some miles on his Chevy, often with his wife Peggy riding shotgun. "She loves it and loves to go for rides," Thomas said. The coupe's odometer now reads 54,000-plus miles, and Thomas has accounted for about 6,000 of those. The Chevy's days of sitting sedentary in a barn appear to be long gone.

"It runs fine, it just doesn't run real fast," Thomas joked. "It's the old babbit-beater engine. It's basically the old oil-splash system. It will run forever as long as you don't over-rap it.

"I get it out when the weather is good. I try to drive it at least once a week. I run across people who'll see the car and say, 'Hey, I remember when Mike's mom used to drive that car.' Some of the old-timers around here remember it."

By Michael Petti

REVISITING THE QUIRKY '38 WILLYS TRUCK

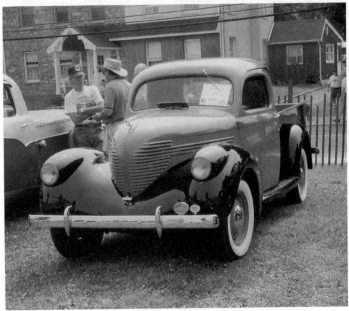

The 1938 Willys pickup was priced at $530, which made
it a bargain compared to most of its competion.

What do the featured 1938 Willys pickup and the 1951 Henry J, 1959 Studebaker Lark and Chrysler's 1981 K-cars (Plymouth Reliant and Dodge Aries) have in common? They are all 175 inches in length.

Now, if you went to the lumberyard for wood, which vehicle would you want? Sure, a standard 2x4 may fit into the wagons of the Lark, Aries and Reliant models if you

open the tailgate and place the 2x4 over the seats and onto the instrument panel. Maybe you could do the same with a Henry J, but what if you wanted to haul plywood? Only the Willys pickup will do, thanks to its 6-foot-long bed.

Today, most Willys trucks haul quarter-mile time slips and speeding tickets as these pickups are often customized or made into hot rods. The appeal of the 1937-'42 Willys

The Willys' rounded front end was very similar to the Willys passenger cars, and the 1938 Grahams.

truck among hot rodders and customizers lies in the truck's light weight, short wheelbase for providing traction and its unique styling shared with Willys automobiles.

Like the 1937 Terraplane pickup or the Studebaker Coupe Express pickups of the same era, the 1937-'42 Willys pickup's front end used passenger-car styling up front, but with a utilitarian truck box in back. Amos Northup designed the 1937 Willys automobile and the 1938 Graham with the same front-end theme. Both grilles were sharply undercut and forward-leaning. While the Willys' hood and grille were rounded, however, the Graham's hood and grille were more angular. On the Graham, at least, the forward-leaning grille was reminiscent of photos depicting early race cars.

The Graham was derisively nicknamed "the sharknose," and hobbyists now refer to any Willys from 1937-'39 as "sharknose" models. The "sharknose" Willys and Graham both have polarizing styling cues — either you love them or hate them.

It has been argued that the 1938 "sharknose" spelled the end for Graham. Willys sales, though, drastically increased in 1937 with the sharknose design, then took a dramatic nosedive in 1938 with the same style. Therefore, it seems more likely that the recession of 1938 hurt Willys and mortally wounded Graham.

In today's parlance, Willys pickups and cars were marketed as entry-level vehicles that undercut the price of the competition. The 1938 Willys pickup was priced at $530, the Ford 60 at $580, the Ford 85 at $590, the Plymouth at $585, the Chevrolet at $592 and the Dodge at $600. Despite its most attractive price, Willys truck sales lagged behind, because for the additional price, other trucks provided many more appealing features.

The 1938 Willys came with a 48-hp four-cylinder while Plymouth, Dodge and Chevrolet offered six-cylinder engines. Ford came with a choice of two V-8 engines. The Model 60 Ford provided 60 hp while the Model 85 generated 85 hp. Dodge, Plymouth, and Chevrolet used modern and safer hydraulic brakes, while Willys and Ford brakes remained the mechanical type.

Ford, Plymouth and Chevrolet trucks each rode a 112-inch wheelbase. Meanwhile, Dodge trucks rode a 116-inch wheelbase and Willys trailed with the shortest wheelbase at 100 inches. This translated into a cramped cabin within the Willys. Something had to give in order to have a 6-foot bed, and so the Willys truck's cabin space suffered. Although marketed as a three-passenger truck, with today's supersized Americans, only two can fit.

Volkswagen Beetle advertisements in the early '60s mentioned numerous changes and improvements for a new model year. However, most people could not tell one model year from another. The same can be said about the Willys pick-up. The only noticeable styling change for 1938 was the elimination of the speed lines on the headlight pods from the 1937 models. Improvements for 1938 included an engine temperature gauge and drip rails over the doors, neither of which were incorporated into 1937 Willys trucks.

Willys club members will note the 1938 Willys pickup is filled with quirks, among them the absence of a voltage regulator (there is only a cutout switch). Also, the carburetor is an unreliable Tillotson; the brake and clutch pedal work from a common pivot; and the factory used two different front fender stampings. One front fender type is a single stamping with a separate headlamp pod while the second fender type has separate front and rear stampings with the front stamping incorporating the headlamp pod into the main stamping.

Driving a Willys truck has additional quirks. Willys pickup's four-cylinder tops out at about 3,200 rpm, and that makes it hard to keep up with highway traffic. The front headlamps and backlight are dim for seeing and being seen. During driving, much steering correction is required, because the Willys is prone to bump-steer, even on slight road irregularities. But, an old truck correctly restored to like-new condition, or an original example with patina, is a three-dimensional portal into the past for future generations to experience first hand.

1930 Cord L29 convertible sedan

1930 Ford Model A convertible coupe

1930 Oldsmobile four-door sedan

1930 Studebaker Dictator Eight rumbleseat coupe

1931 Auburn 8-98 Boattail Speedster

1931 Cadillac Series 370 all-weather phaeton

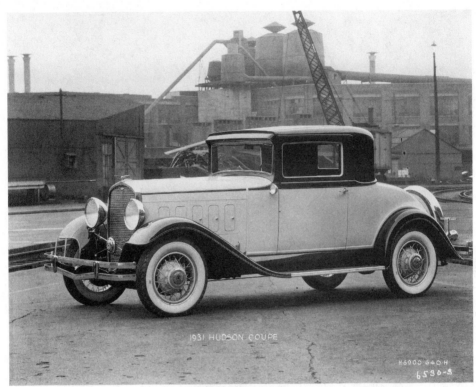

1931 Hudson coupe

1931 GMC 1-ton truck

1931 Chevrolet coupe

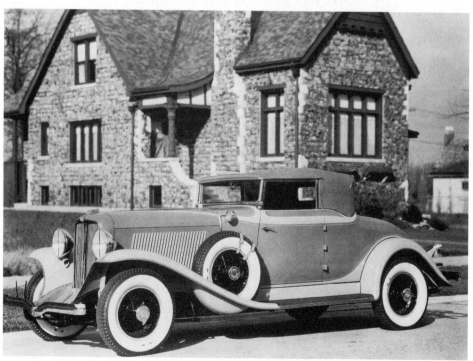

1932 Auburn convertible coupe

1932 Lincoln Model KA closed couple sedan

1932 International-Harvester Model A1 panel truck

1932 Plymouth four-door sedan

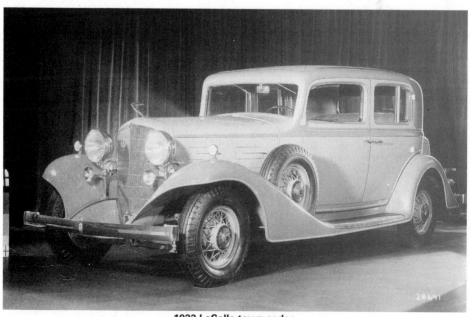

1933 LaSalle town sedan

1933 Chrysler convertible coupe

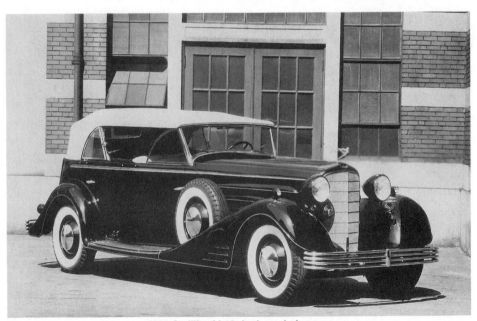

1933 Cadillac V-16 dual-cowl phaeton

1934 Studebaker Dictator roadster

1934 Hupmobile Eight, Series 427 four-door sedan

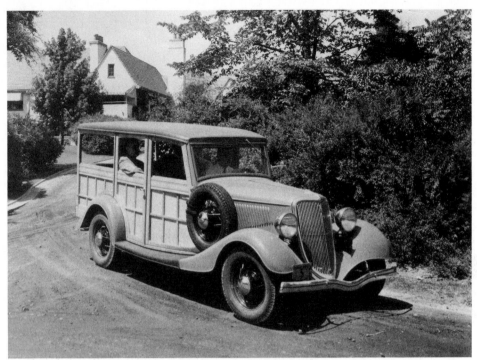

1934 Ford station wagon

1934 Duesenberg SJ dual-cowl phaeton

1935 DeSoto Airflow four-door sedan.

1935 Chevrolet station wagon

1935 Hudson 8 four-door sedan

1936 Ford truck

1936 Pontiac four-door sedan

1936 Buick Roadmaster convertible sedan

1937 Chevrolet Master Deluxe town sedan

1937 Chrysler Airflow four-door sedan

1937 Cadillac Rollston-bodied town car

1937 Lincoln four-door sedan

1937 Dodge Six touring sedan

1938 Oldsmobile four-door sedan

1938 GMC 100 one-ton pickup

1938 Buick Special four-door sedan

1939 Chevrolet four-door sedan

1939 Plymouth convertible sedan

1939 Mercury club coupe

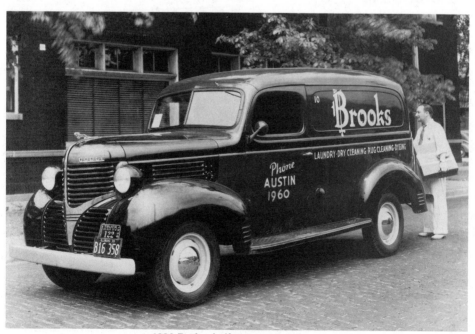

1939 Dodge half-ton panel delivery

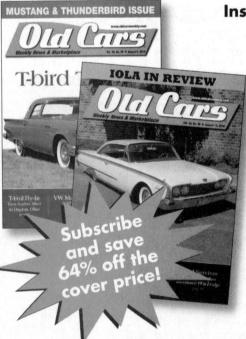

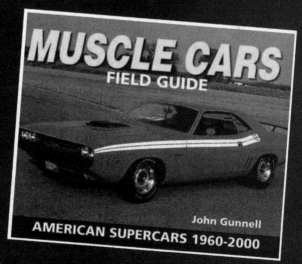